AGRICULTURE-INDUSTRY INTERACTIONS

AGRICULTURE INDUSTRY INTERACTIONS

An Approach to Developing Economies

Editor

Debnarayan Sarkar

KALPAZ

Agriculture-Industry Interactions : An Approach to Developing Economies

Rs. 690

ISBN: 978-81-7835-818-5

Published in 2010 in India by
Kalpaz Publications
C-30, Satyawati Nagar
Delhi-110052
E-mail: kalpaz@hotmail.com
Phone : 9212729499

Laser Type Setting by: Rudra Computer Graphics, Delhi
Printed at : Gian Ridhi Offset Printers, Delhi

Contents

SECTION-3

Preface

At the macroeconomics' level, probably, the most important and most studied relationship in the area of our subject has been the process of interactions between industry and agriculture. The earliest literature dates back to Physiocrats, during the seventeenth century, Francois Quesnay to Madame de Pompadour adored agriculture and regarded it as the only source of wealth. Commerce and industry were regarded merely branches of agriculture. The early masters of political economy like Ricardo, Malthus, and Marx examined the problem from different angles during the nineteenth century. In the 20th century also it has received attention from a diverse body of economists. Bukharin and Preobrazensky studied the problem in the specific context of Soviet industrialization. Kalecki, Lewis, Fei and Ranis, Taylor, and Kador examined it in the context of economic development process.

During the current years one of the most important socio-economic problems leading to violence, causing maximum damage and harm to the people being displaced and uprooted from their socio-cultural milieu, and thereby affecting the stability of the country is the process of transformation from agriculture to industry in a developing country like India. At the core of the politico-economic process of interaction between agriculture and industry due to globalization, privatization and liberalization some pertinent issues arise in the juncture: how far is such process of industrialization for the people, by the people and of the people? How does market play in such a transformation? Thus, the current debate about industrialization is essentially a debate about how the economic and political factors would drive, in an interlocked manner, the transformation of our economy, polity and society.

As a developing economy India finds itself faced with a frontier of development arising out of the transformation from agriculture to industry. Crossing the frontier will definitely not be smooth and benign, and it is only natural for conflicts and disputes to arise. However, the danger lies in these conflicts turning violent and affecting the stability of the country. In such a transformation the rules of the market in many cases (for example, the transfer of land from peasants to private corporations or the rules of the special economic zones) changes in favor of the rich and the powerful. The government has a very crucial role to play in crossing this frontier with minimum damage and harm to the people being displaced. These vital issues are the areas of discussion in this volume. This volume is divided into three Sections: I, II and III. Based on both theoretical foundation and empirical evidences the papers of this volume not only cover various relevant topics related to agriculture-industry interactions or modern-traditional sectors' interactions or formal-informal sectors' interactions but also point out the nature of the market working in practice in such interactions. All these issues would be helpful for academics, students, researchers, practitioners and policy makers interested in development, in addition to being a book of teaching students particularly for macroeconomics, developing economics and political economy.

The editor takes this opportunity to thank profusely all the contributing authors to this volume. More importantly, this volume comes out through the patronage of the University Grants Commission, and I express my deep gratitude to them. I wish to express my deep gratitude to Professor Asis Dasgupta who has inspired me greatly to build up this volume. I am particularly thankful to the non-teaching and library staff of our department, namely, Smt. Suravi Bagchi (Librarian), Sri Swapan Kr. Das, Sri Subrata Das, Ms. Rita Das, Imam Rasul, Sri Balmiki Prasad and Sri Sankar Hela.

Thanks are also due to the publisher of this volume, Kalpaz Publications, and their staff that helped to put it together.

Debnarayan Sarkar
Centre for Economic Studies,
Department of Economics
Presidency College, Kolkata

Introduction

Debnarayan Sarkar

This volume *(Agriculture-Industry Interactive: An Approach to Developing Economies)* introduces together one selected paper in section I, 3 selected papers in section II, both of which incorporate important papers presented in different seminars at the Centre for Economic Studies (CES), and six selected papers in section III, contributed almost by faculty members ,students and research fellows under the Department of Economics, Presidency College, Kolkata. All the selected papers cover various topics related to agriculture-industry interactions or formal-informal interactions or conflict between dual economy and the nature of function of market in such economic conditions. All these are one of the most debatable issues of the developing countries in particular and development perspective in general.

The first paper on section 1 opens with Amit Bhaduri's paper on 'Economic Theory and Ideology: An Approach to Market' delivered in memory of Professor Dipak Banerjee on 6.1.2009 at the CES, Department of Economics, Presidency College, Kolkata. While examining 'Economic Theory and Ideology', Amit Bhaduri exemplifies the ill of the market, which is guided by highly unrealistic assumption leading to an optimum state of affairs in accordance with the dictums of classical liberalism focused exclusively on the individual. The logic of market glorified by neo-liberal economists and politicians drives their process of diversion of natural and other resources to benefit the rich in the name of efficient allocation of resources by the market where millions of children, for example, die of Malaria, Malnutrition, Cholera, TB on the one hand, and create demand for most expensive treatment in the state of art hospital in a highly unequal distribution of income for the rich on the other. In a competitive market all individuals are theoretically equally powerful in carrying out transactions, but the actual rules of the market are embedded in unequal power relations: for instance a small peasant negotiating individually with a giant corporation over his land sale would hardly have equal negotiating power with an Ambani or Tata seeking loan from a bank. Even if powerful market players and financial institutions are threatened with bankruptcy due to their own greed and folly, the market rules are manipulated and bent to suit them, because they are reach and powerful. Even the use of the 'eminent domain' clause to transfer land from peasants to private corporations or the rules for the special economic zones make clear, Bhaduri strongly remarks, how the rules of the game can be changed to alter the very nature of the 'market'; that the government minimizes its social welfare expenditure of all sorts, and the ruthless operation of the market against those who have very little purchasing power continues unabated. He argues that the poor in India, for example, face a double blind with the market, and the state reinforces each other's vicious ruthlessness towards the poor.

In a joint paper titled "Trade Reform, Capital Mobility and Informal Wage in Developing Countries : Theory and Indian Experience" Sugata Marjit and Saibal Kar try to explore the analytical implication of liberal trade policies. Formulating a general equilibrium model of inter-sectoral capital mobility and informal wage, and assuming a two sector open-economy, this paper argues that with limited degree of capital mobility trade reforms reduces the informal wage. But, more importantly, their theoretical model establishes that despite contraction of the formal sector and relocation of labor into the informal segment, the informal wage can still rise if the degree of capital mobility exceeds a critical level. They also offer detailed empirical evidence on the movement of real wages in the informal sector in India explaining the fact that real wage and real fixed assets in the informal manufacturing sector have risen significantly across most States in the post-liberalization period in India. However, in favor of rising real wage in the informal sector, their theoretical explanation lends credence to the fact that the degree of capital mobility between the formal and informal sector is essential for understanding fully the implication of economic reforms on the large informal sectors in the developing world.

While formulating an extended version of the Lewis Model, Amitava Bose's paper –'Lessons from the Lewis Model: Is growth sustainable?' - examines the basic idea of Lewis Model : the long run equilibrium, which involves full-employment, implies that the growth of modern sector is dependent on the use of laborers who are transferred from traditional sector which takes an unlimited supply of unskilled labour. But the impact of globalization in Indian context, he argues, has weakened the link between two internal sectors – traditional and modern – of the country and the changed paradigm of economic development (services, not industry) appears to be giving less importance to abundance of unskilled labor.

In our joint paper (The Way of Industrialization : with Particular Reference to India), Paramgama Sikder, Nikita Modi, Aishani Roy and I try to examine the possible strategies for industrialization necessary for developing countries under the practical framework of the respective countries suited to regional variation of relative factor intensity and relative abundance of factors of production. The strategies for such industrialization aims at increasing the industrial output of the country leading to sustainable regional development as well as reduction of unemployment and that might lead to sustained growth in the standard of living. A theoretical model also appears in the analysis which considers two regions in an economy with differences in relative factor intensity and relative abundance of factors of production, and trade between two such regions takes place. This paper argues that although factor proportion theory is more applicable for cross-country situation, the existing situation of our economy, where both skilled and unskilled labour persist in the economy with the existence of more than one hundred crores of people, production, consumption and exchange of various types of industrial goods are possible across regions or states within our country. This paper might also suggest that such a specialization for different types of industries conducive to different regions may leave open the possibility for gains from increasing returns, usually stemming from falling average costs, from international trade between countries for some manufactured commodities leading to support some modalities of new trade theory (NTT) induced by larger markets and greater specialization in future. But to pave the way for this dynamic expansion induced by larger markets with greater specialization, Government have to comply with some industries' demand for temporarily protection, subsidies and infrastructural investment. This paper also prescribes other necessary measures (infrastructure, education and training, credit, roles of government and NGO's) to make such industrialization more equitable and productive.

I and Debraj Das, in our joint paper titled 'Priority Policy Objectives of West Bengal Left Front Government in the Process of Agriculture-Industry Interactive ', try to formulate a simple theoretical framework of priority-policy objectives for Government of West Bengal in the process of interactions between agriculture and industry of the state of West Bengal in Indian context. This paper also outlines the performance of the Left Front Government of West Bengal during their long ruling period at a stretch they started in 1977. This study, however, suggests that in the process of agriculture-industry interactions, West Bengal Left Front Government have been lying much below the critical level of satisfying their prime-policy objectives (employment generation, increase in income and poverty reduction) during their long period of journey.

Mousumi Dutta and S. Satyabhama, in their paper titled "Regional Variation in Occupational Segregation in India : Some Evidence from NSS Data" address the issue of gender-based occupational segregation, which is one of the most important factors contributing to inequality between labor market around the world, due to impact of policies of liberalization and globalization, addressing several issues related to women-workforce participation, they analyze the trend involved in gender-based job-segregation in India in non-agricultural sector over the recent years based on the data of urban sectors for two time-periods : 1993-94 and 1999-2000. Their study reveals that female-labour force in the non-agricultural sector in India receives low wage-rate. Despite a gradual rise in the share of women in the total non-agricultural work-force, such a segregation does not lead to any tendency towards feminization of labour in the 1990s. This study, however, suggests that, among others increased educational attainment among women may open up new occupational avenues for women to join the non-agricultural work-force.

In his paper titled "The Nexus between Agricultural Prices and Industrial Prices in India: A time-series study", Rajnarayan Gupta investigates into causality between the prices of primary articles and manufactured products in India. His study, which considers standard time-series technique, finds no causality in either direction; price level of primary articles and that of manufactured products move independently of each other.

Amitava Chatterjee's paper (The Interaction between Agriculture and Industry with Reference to the Current Indian Scenario) outlines some problems and prospects of Indian Economy in the process of interaction between agriculture and industry. He points out both growth and human development issues in the process of interactions. Interpersonal comparisons of utility cannot really be avoided, he argues, to spread over its benefits for a long period of time.

In the article entitled 'Economic development in the shadows of Socio-political conflicts: An agenda for West Bengal', Avijit Dutta provides a survey of conflict theory from economic and socio-political viewpoints and attempts to collate those theoretical premises. He also suggests a scheme of empirical research in the context of West Bengal using the notion of conflict, which in his perception, the right framework for the analysis of the present interaction and tension generated by the industrialization process.

In our joint paper titled 'Growth, Regional Pattern and Performance of Food Processing Industry in West Bengal' I, Madhuchhanda Saha and Indrani Basu attempt to make an assessment of the status of food-processing industry in the state of West Bengal. Looking at the comparative growth of food and non-food industries, the study finds, it is observed that the food industry has become more capital intensive. Increase in NVA has positive and significant effect on the capital intensity in the industry in the industry as is evident from the regression analysis that evinces that growth in NVA causes more increase in FC than in employment. This implies that a high growth achieved in NVA during 1981-82 to 1997-98 has increased capital intensity in the industry. The employment growth in the industry has been largely due to addition of new factories, not because of increase in employment intensity. The assessment of relative efficiency reflects that the food-industry did not perform well during the period under consideration.

This volume, however, addresses, in a modest way, those issues on development perspectives particularly for developing countries, which are advocated on the grounds of sustained economic growth and employment, policies towards trade reform, capital mobility between formal and informal sectors, informal wage structure, price structure between agricultural and industrial commodities, strategies towards industrialization suited to regional variation of relative factor intensity and relative abundance of factors of production, wage structure for gender based occupational segregation in the non-agricultural sector, agriculture-industry interaction and priority policy objectives and the like. Moreover, this volume also exemplifies the ill of the market structure in practice to such dynamics. All the papers of this volume appear in a logical sequence. All these are one of the most debatable issues of the developing countries in particular and development perspective in general. Due to its comprehensiveness and contemporariness, it is felt that this volume would be useful for academics, students, researchers, practitioners and policy makers interested in development, in addition to being a book of teaching students particularly for macroeconomics, developing economics and political economy.

List of Contributors

Dr. Amit Bhaduri

Professor Emeritus, Centre for Economic Studies and Planning, Jawaharlal Nehru University, New Delhi.

Visiting Professor: Professor of Political Economy, University of Pavia.

Ex. Professor : Institute of Management, Calcutta, Delhi School of Economics and Jawaharlal Nehru University, Delhi, and Centre for Development Studies, Trivandrum, El College de Mexico, Stanford University, U.S.A., Vienna and Linz University, Austria, Norwegian University of Science and Technology, Bremen University, Germany, Bologna and Pavia University, Italy.

He has also been a Fellow of various Institutes of Advanced Studies in Austria, Sweden, Germany and Italy, worked on various expert bodies of the United Nations, and served as member on some national and international commissions.

Dr. Amitava Bose

Professor, Indian Institute of Management, Kolkata.

Former Director : Indian Institute of Management, Kolkata.

Ex. Professor: Cornell University, U.S.A., Calcutta University, Indian Statistical Institute, Kolkata.

Dr. Sugata Marjit

Director, Centre for Studies in Social Science, Kolkata and

R.B.I. Professor of Industrial Economics.

Visiting Professor: Cornell University, U.S.A, University of Florida, Pennsylvania State University, University of Rochester, U.S.A.

Ex. Professor: Indian Statistical Institute, Kolkata, Jadavpur University, CESP, Jawaharlal Nehru University, New Delhi.

Dr. Saibal Kar

Research Fellow, Centre for Studies in Social Studies, Kolkata.

Dr. Debnarayan Sarkar

Professor and Secretary, Centre for Studies in Social Science, Kolkata.

Aishani Roy

Student, 3rd Year (Hons.), Department of Economics, Presidency College, Kolkata.

B.Sc. (Hons.) Economics (Part 1):1st Class First, University of Calcutta.

Award: Goldman Sachs world leader award, 2009 (Goldman Sachs Foundation).

Nikita Modi

Student, 3rd Year (Hons.), Department of Economics, Presidency College, Kolkata.

B.Sc. (Hons.) Economics (Part 1):High 1st Class Marks, University of Calcutta.

Parangama Sikdar
Student, 3rd Year (Hons.), Department of Economics, Presidency College, Kolkata.
B.Sc. (Hons.) Economics (Part 1): High 1st Class Marks, University of Calcutta.

Debraj Das
Junior Research Fellow, Centre for Economic Studies, Presidency College, Kolkata.

Dr. Mousumi Dutta
Reader, Department of Economics, Presidency College, Kolkata.

Dr. Rajnarayan Gupta
Reader, Department of Economics, Presidency College, Kolkata.

Amitava Chatterjee
Professor and Head, Department of Economics, Presidency College, Kolkata.

Avijit Dutta
Senior Lecturer, Department of Economics ,Presidency College, Kolkata.
Senior Research Fellow : Indian Statistical Institute, Kolkata,1991.

Madhuchhanda Saha
M.Sc., Department of Economics, Presidency College, Kolkata, 2008.

Indrani Basu
Junior Research Fellow, Centre for Economic Studies, Presidency College, Kolkata.

SECTION - I

1

Economic Theory and Ideology: An Approach to Market

Amit Bhaduri

(Lecture delivered in memory of Professor Dipak Banerjee on 6.1.2009) Presidency College, Calcutta)

The topic I have chosen for this lecture, I think would have been of mutual interest in a rather special sense to both Professor Dipak Banerjee and to me. Professor Banerjee was by temperament a logician who happened to be interested also in economic theory for its internal consistency and logical elegance. He did not mix up his love for theory with ideology because he knew the two did not mix easily. He was also a man of exceptional personal and intellectual integrity. I came to appreciate it increasingly over time as we continued to admire his courageous stand with his colleague Professor Mihir Rakshit about the need to maintain the high standard of undergraduate teaching in economics for which Presidency College, Calcutta had become famous world over. The education policy of the state government was not compatible with it, and Professor Banerjee did not compromise for convenience. He had the courage to be in the minority of one so long as he knew he was right. In a way he displayed the same courageous attitude of a man guided by reason when it came to the uses and abuses of economic theory in practical situations. He was wary of supporting political ideologies in so far as they required unreasonable faith. However he was forthright, as I recall from a specific incident in early 1990s, in calling the bluff when others talked unreasonably of economic ideology devoid of logic. Thus, he was equally unforgiving in his criticism of vulgar Marxism and of vulgar market fundamentalism. And his personal integrity became a matter of admiration for us all, when he took public stand against powerful adversaries like the Left United Front on higher education policy, and the IMF 'conditionalities' through a loan to India (The protest of a group of Indian economists had been organized by late Professor Iqbal Gulati).

Through occasional discussion, (usually in form of 'addas') extending over many years I came to appreciate the essence of his attitude to economic theory. Economic propositions derived logically from precisely stated assumptions or axioms are seldom guides to policy. They are mostly in the nature of precautionary knowledge, in so far as they caution us against claiming too much on the basis of theory. And, this can a double edged weapon as Banerjee's attitude clearly exemplified. He stood up, when necessary alone, as he saw that many pronouncements by both the Left- and the Right-oriented economists was devoid of reason, but pretended to be derived from economic theory. In the last few years of his life, he was acutely aware how in the name of economic theory, but without any real theoretical basis, our previous understanding of the functions of the state and of the society was being replaced by standards set by the market. All major political parties across the spectrum from the Right to the Left succumbed to it willingly or unwillingly until the recent economic crisis. When in power, their actions spoke louder than words, and these actions are apparently intended at replacing the failures of the state by the efficiency of the market. However, what is the nature of this 'market' that is at the core of this ideology? Economic theory might help to clarify matters a little. Banerjee would have used high powered theory of Arrow-Debreu general equilibrium to drive home the point. However, we might agree to reason out for the present purpose in simplified terms.

We all know markets involve various buying and selling activities organized under certain rules. By and large, economists study in great detail the properties of an abstract form of the market called perfect competition. Under highly unrealistic assumptions that make the perfectly competitive market an almost mythical form of idealized competition, it is shown that an equilibrium set of prices exist which simultaneously clears all markets by equating demand and supply. Moreover, these prices are shown to result in an efficient and (Pareto-) optimum arrangement where no individual participant in the market can do better. So, this is an optimum state of affairs in accordance with the dictums of classical liberalism focused exclusively on the individual.

The mythical notion of perfect competition has created the powerful ideological metaphor of the 'invisible hand' of the market leading a society of self seeking individuals to an optimum state. This would imply two things. First, selfishness without any concern for the collective becomes an unintended social virtue, because the society can reach an optimum through the individual's self-centered activities in the market. Margaret Thatcher, a former conservative prime minister of Britain famously echoed this sentiment by claiming that there is no society, only individuals! Second, because the unregulated competitive market is claimed to achieve an optimum, any regulatory role of the government become redundant, even counter-productive in many instances (This view too was made academically more respectable with the award of several Nobel Memorial prizes in economics). Aided by such theories, driving for a minimalist role for the state becomes the war cry of various versions of neo-liberalism.

Nevertheless, the virtues of even this mythical model of perfect competition remain flawed in so far as it does not guarantee that the distribution of income in the society would be tolerably acceptable to all its members despite the Pareto optimality! To appreciate its practical implications, remember demand depends on the purchasing power of the participants in any market. Thus an unequal distribution of income even under competitive conditions might mean millions of children dying from malnutrition, or from easily preventable and treatable diseases like cholera, malaria or T.B. At the same time, a highly unequal distribution of income would create demand for most expensive treatments in state of the art hospitals for the rich (and even for the treatment of obesity from plain over-eating). This is indeed inherent in the logic of the market, because voting takes place in the market according to purchasing power. Thus, a handful of rich would have many more 'votes' than millions of poor in determining what would be profitable to produce for the market. Greater scope for the market in India today means villages go without housing, sanitation and drinkable water, but selected areas of cities pride themselves with world class amenities of luxury hotels, apartments, and malls. The logic of the market glorified by neo-liberal economists and politicians drives this process of diversion of natural and other resources to benefit the rich in the name of efficient allocation of resources by the market.

Outside the charmed circle of a few theoretical economists it is seldom emphasized that, without additional stringent assumptions economic theory does not guarantee neither even the local stability, let alone a sufficiently high speed of convergence to such a competitive equilibrium (For a non-technical version the reader may consult, "The intrinsic limits of modern economic theory: the emperor has no clothes" by Alan Kirman, *Economic Journal,* conference, 1989, Vol. 99, pp.126-139). In simpler language this means that we have no idea in general about whether market equilibrium is attainable, and how long it might take to converge (if it at all does) to the optimum state. And here lies a political trick that practical pro-reform politicians often play. A neo-liberal prime minister or his pro-market finance minister can always claim that economic reforms are working well, and are about to produce results, perhaps with some more reforms, but they cannot specify even in theory, let alone in actual practice, the time needed for achieving the desired results. Like a dictator, the competitive market is without accountability within any definite time frame, and can go on promising without delivering! However, political democracy unlike the market system has some built-in accountability and, there is usually some reckoning at the time of elections. I need only to remind you that market based reformers repeatedly did badly on that count. The slogan of "shining India" crashed in the last (2004) general election, and the present Prime Minister, widely considered a guru of India's market oriented reforms, could not ever personally win an election. No wonder, come election time and the enthusiasm for reforms fades, gone election time and it is back in business justifying the quip, "the masses vote but the class rules".

It needs hardly saying that actual markets are far removed from the mythical state of affairs depicted by perfect competition. In a competitive market all individual participants are equally powerful in carrying out transactions. It is an error, deliberate or otherwise, to assume that the actual rules of the market, unlike that of perfect competition, are impersonal and anonymous. In contrast, actual market transactions are embedded in unequal power relations. For instance, a starving agricultural labourer wanting a consumption loan from his local money lender is very differently placed from an Ambani or a Tata seeking loan from a bank. In this context it is especially important to remember that a small peasant negotiating individually with a giant corporation over his land sale would hardly have equal negotiating power. Since land and the associated natural resources like water, forest and minerals involve the livelihood of multitudes, it becomes in many ways analogous to selling labour power. There is an obvious danger in treating land and labour simply as commodities meant for exchange like other commodities. This was perhaps the reason why Karl Polanyi in his classic, "The Great Transformation" called them 'fictitious commodities'. When manipulated by grossly unequal market power relations, these fictitious commodities have wide repercussions on the citizens of a country, calling for counter-action by the state as a part of a grand 'double movement' between the market and the state. However, rather than being moderated, these embedded market power relations often tend to be exacerbated systematically by government policies in the name of market oriented reforms. The rules are manipulated and bent to suit the rich and powerful. To take only one example, the World Bank and the IMF imposed on developing countries various market oriented reforms, privatization programmes and reduction in government activities as 'conditionalities' for loans. This usually had the implicit, and occasionally explicit support of the U.S. government. And yet, when powerful market players in the U.S. like large banks and financial institutions are threatened with bankruptcy due to their own greed and folly (as in the recent housing mortgage triggered crisis in 2008), all market based rules and disciplines are questioned to justify a massive rescue operation by a government that had preached free market rules and policies as great virtues to others!

The most pervasive fallout of this market centric ideology is the least noticed. It has created the tendency to treat the market, not a human institution but almost as the natural state of our economic and social existence. It has resulted in the greatest ideological displacement of our time. Through a chorus of pronouncements of interested politicians, academics, and corporate controlled media, this has largely succeeded in crippling our traditional understanding of the state as a regulator and moderator of the forces of the market against the poor. Those who are powerful enough to manipulate the rules by which the market is organized, claim most loudly that the market can guide or even act as a substitute for our moral values. Thus, making loss is considered a 'bad' thing in general, while making profit is treated as a 'good' thing irrespective of what is being produced, or for whom it is being produced. For example, there is continuous pressure for the privatization of most essential utilities like water, basic health, and education which means in effect the poor has to buy these services in the market irrespective of their ability to pay. It is called public-private partnership by the World Bank these days where the public sector bears most the risk and the private sector takes most of the profit. The use of the 'eminent domain' clause to transfer land from peasants to private corporation, or the rules for the Special Economic Zones make clear how the rules of the game can be changed to alter the very nature of the 'market'.

The logic of the market is let loose on the overwhelming majority of India's poor. Close to 42 per cent of the population is poor by internationally set definition of absolute poverty on a latest World Bank count, and over three fourths of the population are poor with purchasing power of less than rupees 20 a day according to another source. It must be remembered that they have little voice in the market in terms of purchasing power, whereas a handful rich can dominate the market. Yet, by attributing an almost moral dimension to the functioning of the market mechanism the pro-market logic undermines our political democracy of one adult one vote, and the market continues to discriminate systematically against the poor by increasing inequality in the society through three major routes.

The high growth in output at an average rate of some 7 per cent over the last two decades has resulted in regular employment growth hardly exceeding 1 per cent. The rest of the average 6 percent growth in GDP came from the growth in output per worker or labour productivity. In contrast, during the earlier decades, when GDP grew on an average at less than 4 per cent, regular employment grew at the annual rate of 2 per cent. The recent drive to increase labour productivity has an international aspect. Globalisation in trade means increasing the importance of the external compared to the internal market. Corporations can compete in the world market mostly by cutting costs to increase their international competitiveness while maintaining quality. Above all, this means shedding labour force through mechanisation to increase productivity, in addition to restraining wages through labour contracts unfavourable to the workers. For instance, if the labour force in a corporation is downsized to half at the same wage, labour cost per unit of output would be also be halved. How this process is working in practice can be glimpsed from a few specific cases. Edward Luce of *Financial Times* (London) reported that the Jamshedpur Steel Plant of the Tatas employed 85000 workers in 1991 to produce1 million tons of steel worth 0.8 million U.S. dollars. In 2005, the production rose to 5 million tons, worth about 5 million U.S. dollars, while employment fell to just about half. Despite being two of the lagest receivers of direct foreign investment and housing most of India's big corporate houses, Gujarat and Maharashtra were among the slowest growing states in terms of regular income generation (*Times of India* headlined this information on 7 July, 2008 based on 61st NSS report). Employment in regular jobs increased far too slowly leaving most Indians in the Hell described by the great Italian poet Dante. On the gate of his imagined Hell is written, "This is the land you enter after abandoning all hopes."

At the same time, the government is unwilling to increase expenditure on social services to soften the ruthlessness of the market mechanism. Instead, it follows a policy of 'prudent' sound finance by not letting fiscal deficit increase too much. Thus, the percentage of government expenditure on both health and education in this overwhelmingly poor country remained stagnant at slightly over 1 and 2 per cent of GDP respectively, and the poorest with no other alternative are hit hardest by such austerity of government policy. And despite much publicity, the fate of a truncated and bureaucratized Employment Guarantee Scheme, the Integrated Child Development Programme or, of the targeted Public Distribution System has hardly been better. The indirect adverse impact of such policies persists over time due to the ill health and ill education of the younger generations. The government continues to talk of India as an emerging global economic power, while the poor continue to suffer, leaving more than half the children grossly under nourished and without any education.

The apparent reasons given for nearly stagnant spending on social services are lack of 'money' and poor public delivery system of social services. However, the more compelling reason is the globalisation of finance that has made the government highly sensitive to the moods of the stock market and the financial sentiments of major players in that market. India has a relatively large foreign exchange reserve (It was close to 300 billion U.S. dollars before the economic crisis in September 2008).However, unlike China which has been enjoying export surplus for years, our reserve comes mostly from capital inflows exceeding balance of payments deficits, like deposits from NRIs, portfolio investments by various international banks and financial institutions. These deposits are mostly foot-loose by nature, and can be withdrawn at relatively short notice if the mood of the financial market turns sour. The government tries to guard against this danger of possible large scale capital flight by being on the right side of the IMF and the World Bank because they have a central role in shaping international financial opinion for banks, credit-rating agencies, and other financial institutions. This means following their guidelines in formulating economic policies. Thus, the government minimises its social welfare expenditure of all sorts, and the ruthless operation of the market against those with very little purchasing power continues unabated. The cost of this squeeze on public expenditure through lack of social security, education, health and nutrition is borne mostly by the poor who are excluded increasingly from the market due to lack of job opportunities. The poor in India face a double blind with the market and the state reinforcing each other's vicious ruthlessness towards the poor.

Land acquisition for mining, industrialisation and SEZ together has turned the indirect into a direct assault on the poor. The destruction of agriculture based livelihood deepens the extreme despair in this already bleak situation. Farmers continue to commit suicide in thousands; at least one fourth of land mass covering over 125 districts of the country in twelve states is witnessing steady growth of extremist (naxalite) activities. The Adivasis (8 per cent) and the Dalits (16 per cent) accounting for almost 25 per cent of India's population remain among its poorest on almost all accounts. And yet, they have all along been the biggest victim of the form of developmental terrorism through land acquisition by the state. Of 25 million hectares used for all development projects since 1947 to 2000, nearly half used to be common land accessed by Adivasi communities and forest dwellers, the Dalits and the poorest in India for supplementing their meager livelihood. The common land used for 'national' development deprived systematically these people of their livelihood. Thus, at least 40 per cent of the displaced persons are Adivasis who constitute no more than 8 per cent of the population (Data collected by Dr. Walter Fernandes).

This provides the background to our process of economic expansion which benefits not more than 25 per cent of our population. It is being sustained by the rapidly growing purchasing power of this minority. It has led to a mutually reinforcing vicious mechanism by which higher growth leads to greater inequality, and greater inequality feeds on higher growth. Guided by market profitability, resource allocation becomes biased against the poor as the composition of incremental output through growth changes in favour of the rich who can pay. The poor becomes a low priority for the market as well as for the government in the name of economic development. To celebrate this as the regime of high growth and India's emergence as a global economic power is a cruel joke on the poor majority of this country. The joke has begun to turn a little sour even for the rich with the onslaught of the engulfing economic crisis and that might not be a bad thing altogether if it forces a change in the direction of our economic policies.

SECTION - II

2

Trade Reform, Capital Mobility and Informal Wage in Developing Countries : Theory and Indian Evidence

Sugata Marjit and Saibal Kar

Acknowledgements

This research is supported by a financial grant (Grant No: 05-RG-10234) from the Poverty and Economic Policy (PEP) Network, Canada. Sugata Marjit is indebted to seminar and conference participants at the Middle East and North Africa Unit of the World Bank, Indian Statistical Institute, University of Sydney, CSSSC, Nobuhiro Kiyotaki, Ronald Jones and Mukul Majumdar for comments. Saibal Kar thanks Ira Gang, Kunal Sen and participants at ESRC Conference, UEA; PEP conferences in Colombo and Addis Ababa for helpful comments. The usual disclaimer applies.

The purpose of this paper is to explore the analytical implications of liberal trade policies on the real wage of informal workers. The term 'informal sector' as initially coined by ILO (1972) refers to, "illicit or illegal activities by individuals operating outside the formal sphere for the purpose of evading taxation or regulatory burden." It may alternatively be defined as, "very small enterprises that use low-technology models and do not refer to legal status" (Webster & Fidler, 1996). Although dominantly, the informal sector activity pertains to non-traded items in the economy, from small retailers and street vendors to domestic helps, in many developing countries they produce exportable and import substitutes either independently or with subcontracting from the formal sector. In its own rights, the informal sector has become an institution in all developing and transition countries with various positive and negative implications it generates (for example, Davis, 2006 argues that division of labour becomes greater than optimal in the presence of informal institutions, resulting in greater than optimal complexity and higher growth in the economy).

On an average, about 70% of the labour force in the LDCs belongs to the informal sector. Data from Southeast Asian, East European, African, and Latin American countries show varying rates of urban informal sector employment with a range going up from 15% to 20% in Turkey and Slovakia to 80% in Zambia, or even more, to about 83% in Myanmar. Moreover, considering the state of agricultural and rural activities in these countries, it is quite apparent that the total share of the informal sector in the economy as a whole would be very high (ILO, 1999). This is corroborated by some of the other studies, for example Turnham (1993), which provide evidence that in low-income countries like Nigeria, Bangladesh, Ivory Coast, India, and elsewhere, the share of the urban informal sector is at least as high as 51%. The informal labour market, characterized by competitive wage formation rather than unionized process of negotiations, has subsequently emerged as an important institution in the entire developing world. Agenor (1996) and references therein provide ample evidence testifying the predominance of informal labour markets in the entire developing world.

Alternatively, seen from the point of view of the 'minimum wage' earners, only 11% of Tunisia's labour force is subject to minimum wage; in Mexico and Morocco, a substantive number earns less than the minimum wage; in Taiwan, minimum wage is less than half of the average wage and so on (Agenor, 1996). Interestingly, in the so-called informal sector many workers earn even less than the minimum wage, typically because the existence of non-market clearing downward rigid wages along with other corporate taxes pushes many private firms to operate in the informal sector (see Gang and Gangopadhyay, 1990 for further discussion and evidence on this).

The case of India offers a glaring example in this context. An overwhelmingly large proportion (approximately 93%) of the industrial and service sector workforce in India is employed under informal arrangements. A substantial portion of such employment opportunities is generated in the urban or semi-urban areas and not surprisingly a majority of this workforce is economically marginalized. High incidence of poverty among these groups exposed to difficult and hazardous working conditions, non-existent social security or health benefit schemes other than poorly functioning state-provided medical facilities, and etc., is quite common. Contrary to conventional belief, it is also witnessed that despite economic prosperity private firms and recently even public organizations are entering into informal employment contracts, where workers receive contractual tenures and wages, with no access to various benefits that earlier generation of workers enjoyed. Dwindling labour union presence in many institutions have also contributed strongly in favour of such hiring practices. While these refer to informal practices within the formal institutions, a larger group of workers face more pervasive informalization, with enormous implications it has on aspects of income volatility, poverty and standard of living for all inside and outside the informal segment. Given the economic trends in most developing countries, it is inconceivable that the size of the informal sector would shrink considerably below the existing level and therefore, sustained improvements in the living standards of these groups can only be brought about by capital accumulation, productivity gains and wage increase in this sector.

While there are several mechanisms that can generate such positive economic impact for the existing group, here we argue that one of the crucial factors in this category is the *degree of capital mobility* between the formal and the informal sectors. The motivation behind invoking the issue of capital mobility comes from the observation that several developing countries have been experimenting with policies on trade reform for quite some time, wherein the critical feature has been the contraction of the formal protected industries, either via import liberalization or through state initiatives in withdrawing support from loss-making public enterprises. This implies that a large amount of capital and labour that were earlier part of these industries would now have to relocate to a more profitable venture. It should be noted that in most of these countries, the vacuum left by the vanishing large scale public industries have been filled not by similar manufacturing units, but by a predominantly service oriented industrial structure which face less stringent labour laws and industrial regulations. And moreover, the new opportunities that have emerged in the so-called sunshine industries are incapable of accommodating the retrenched capital and labour, a larger share of which has hence been devoted to less formal applications. There may be several explanations for this transition, which include the fact that workers in typical import-competing public or private enterprises would not find an easy access to the more formal service industries, which require high-skilled professionals with certain technical expertise, that these old industries rarely employed.

This would further mean that an assessment of the success of trade reform in poor countries is incomplete without an explicit account of the welfare of the informal workers and of the capital owners who have relocated to riskier and supposedly more profitable businesses. Obviously, the prime concern in this context is the economic return an informal worker receives when more such workers are involuntarily retrenched from the formal sector and crowd into the informal counterpart. In fact, a critical stance against downsizing artificially bloated and subsidized formal sector is supported by an argument that such downsizing will drive labour into the informal sector, lowering wages and forcing workers to survive in poorer working conditions. If one assumes diminishing marginal productivity of labour, a larger work force, *ceteris paribus*, must mean lower real wage. This is the usual partial equilibrium response one should expect. However, the general equilibrium outcomes could be quite different. For example, if the displaced workforce is accompanied by fresh investments in the informal sector, existing informal workers are likely to gain. In the present paper, we argue why mobility of capital is essential for understanding fully the implications of economic reform on the large informal sectors in the developing world and in particular, one of the contributions of this paper lies in establishing that despite contraction of the formal sector and relocation of labour into the informal segment the informal wage can still rise if the degree of capital mobility exceeds a critical level.

2. Literature Review and Specific Objectives

Both theoretically and empirically we highlight the role of capital mobility between the formal and the informal sectors in determining the direction of the informal wage, when the formal segment is adversely affected by liberal trade policies. The theoretical piece offers distinct departures from the traditional literature that uses the Harris-Todaro type structures to model informal sector (for example, Fields 1975;

Gupta, 1993, 1997; etc.). However, problems with the Harris-Todaro framework are now well known (Basu, 1984; and Majumdar, 1976, 1983), and a critique of the structure is that open unemployment among the poor workers is far less plausible than conjectured, since remaining unemployed for long involves severe costs for such groups. Therefore, it is quite likely that they settle for any job, most of which are located in the informal sector. When the sector faces an excess supply of such workers, crashing of wages than unemployment, are more feasible outcomes. Using this very realistic phenomenon in the developing world, our theoretical framework uses a full-employment model, where wage in the formal sector is set at a high level by unionized bargaining while the informal segment faces a low flexible wage. The theoretical inspirations behind this framework are drawn from Carruth and Oswald (1981), Agenor and Montiel (1996), Kar and Marjit (2001), Marjit and Beladi (2002) and Marjit (2003), etc. It should be noted, however, that the present paper is substantially different from an earlier work by Marjit (2003), where the informal sector supplies an intermediate good to the formal sector and that capital mobility is not modeled explicitly. The present paper not only offers a more general approach on the issue but also derives the exact condition of capital mobility that in turn affects the conditions in the informal sector. Therefore, the present study is a significant improvement on the understanding of the interaction between capital flows and wages earned by unskilled labour in a developing country context.

Moreover, unlike previous studies, here we bring in imperfections in the allocation of existing stock of capital between the formal and the informal manufacturing. Albeit, the informal sector may not use up a vast amount of capital itself because of inadequate property rights or due to the absence of contractual protections, there is evidence of some degree of intersectoral mobility of capital.[1] Essentially, therefore we model the mobility of capital explicitly, which depends on return differential and that the inability of capital to relocate affects the accumulation process in the informal segment. If capital is guaranteed of a protected return in the formal sector, it hardly has any reason to flow out to the informal counterpart. However, as the protectionary shelter is withdrawn, capital relocates where it continues earning the highest returns. In certain cases, such movements could be a lengthy process and quite costly, depending on existing institutional arrangements.

The empirical basis of our theoretical work is drawn from the evidence on informal wage and capital accumulation in the informal manufacturing sector in India. We use various rounds (1984-85, 1989-90, 1994-95, 1999-00 and 2000-01) of National Sample Survey data to demonstrate: (1) the real informal wage for the non-directory manufacturing enterprise (NDME) has increased between the pre-reform and the post-reform decades; (2) real capital stock in the organized manufacturing has remained stagnant or declined in real terms vis-à-vis real fixed assets in the informal sector that has grown substantially in the post-reform period; (3) For majority of the states and union territories in India, the growth of real informal wage is significantly explained by growth of real fixed assets and real value added in the informal sector.

While we are not building up a model to explain the movement in the real informal wage in India, our theoretical work highlights the case of rising informal wage in accordance with a rising capital stock in the informal sector. We argue that if trade reform reduces the output of the import-competing product and subsequently drives labor to the informal sector, the informal wage tends to *rise* only when a 'critical' amount of capital also relocates to the informal sector alongside labor. In a static general equilibrium model this is captured by a greater allocation of capital in the informal sector and a simultaneous decline in the capital stock in the formal counterpart. While direct empirical evidence can hardly capture this mobility, we use a proxy estimates to demonstrate that there have been phases in post-reform India when capital in the organized manufacturing did not grow at all. However, during the same periods, real fixed assets – a true measure of capital stock - in the informal sector grew substantially. We use this evidence as a plausible, rather a concrete, foundation for our theoretical propositions.

Our paper has a strong policy implication. If intersectoral capital flow is severely restricted by institutional and other factors, downsizing of the formal segment will be harmful to the vast majority of informal workers. Excess supply of labor in the informal sector must be accompanied by adequate investments in this sector in order for informal workers to benefit.

The third section develops the theoretical model. The fourth offers empirical evidence and section 5 concludes.

3. The Model

We assume a two-sector small open economy. X is produced in the formal manufacturing sector and Y is the informal manufacturing sector. Both X and Y use labor and capital. Wage in the formal segment is fixed through bargaining. Initially, X is protected either through a tariff or by a state-subsidy, which artificially increases the price of X. Trade reform or withdrawal of subsidy implies a decline in the tariff/subsidy rate, denoted by t. Workers, who do not find jobs in the formal sector flock in sector Y where they receive the market determined wage rate. We call this the informal wage. There is no open unemployment in this model. People must find jobs to survive, and wage in the informal sector adjusts fully to accommodate workers moving into the sector. Markets are competitive and technology exhibits CRS and diminishing marginal productivity.

The model is similar in spirit to Agenor and Montiel (1996), Carruth and Oswald (1981), Marjit and Beladi (2002) and Marjit (2003). Capital and land are fully employed.

The symbols we use are given as follows:

$\overline{w}$: Formal unionized wage; w : Informal (flexible) wage

r_i : Return to capital in sector i; X : Output of formal sector;

Y : Output of informal sector; (P_X, P_Y) : Exogenous commodity prices

$\overline{L}$: Supply of Labor; $\overline{K}$: Total supply of capital

K_i : Supply of capital in sector i, where $i = X, Y$.; (a_{LX}, a_{LY}) : Per unit labor use in X and Y.

(a_{KX}, a_{KY}) : Per unit capital use in X and Y; t : Tariff rate or subsidy.

'^' represents percentage changes for particular variables and symbols used bear the same implications as in Jones (1965).

Competitive price equations that describe the system are given by,

$$\overline{w}a_{LX} + r_X a_{KX} = P_X(1+t) \tag{1}$$

$$wa_{LY} + r_Y a_{KY} = P_Y \tag{2}$$

Commodity prices are given from the rest of the world. Let us suppose Y is exported and X is imported.

Full employment conditions imply:

$$a_{LX}X + a_{LY}Y = \overline{L} \tag{3}$$

$$K_X + K_Y = \overline{K} \tag{4}$$

$$a_{KX}X = K_X \tag{5}$$

$$a_{KY}Y = K_Y \tag{6}$$

Let $\hat{\bar{w}}$ be so determined that,

$$\hat{\bar{w}} = \alpha \hat{P}_X + \beta \hat{P}_Y, \quad 0 < \alpha, \beta < 1 \tag{7}$$

Finally, the capital mobility condition:

$$\frac{K_X}{K_Y} = \phi\left(\frac{r_X}{r_Y}\right), \phi' > 0 \tag{8}$$

Equation (8) suggests the following. At any point of time $\overline{K}$ is allocated between *X* and *Y*. But such allocation depends on return differential. Hence there is imperfect mobility of capital. If $\left(\frac{r_X}{r_Y}\right)$, increases, $\frac{K_X}{K_Y}$ will also increases. $\frac{K_X}{K_Y}$ describes the relative supply of capital in sector *X*. The usual way to model this is to assume sector-specific capital for *X* and *Y* without any mobility with $\phi' = 0$. Perfect mobility will always imply $r_Y = r_X$ and there is no relevance for a separate sectoral supply function of capital. Relative supply adjusts to demand in each sector and this is the standard Heckscher-Ohlin structure. We shall demonstrate that our comparative static depends on the curvature of $\phi' = 0$.

Given $(P_X + t, P_Y)$, $\overline{w}$, *L*, and *K*, we have w, r_X, r_Y, *X*, *Y*, K_X, K_Y to solve from (1)-(6) and (8). The determination of general equilibrium proceeds as follows. From (1) we can determine. Now using (4) and (8) we get (8)$'$.

$$\frac{\overline{K} - K_Y}{K_Y} = \phi\left(\frac{r_X}{r_Y}\right)$$

As r_Y increases, given r_X and $\phi' > 0$, K_Y must rise. This defines the relationship *MM* in figure (1). Now using (5), (6) and (3),

$$\frac{a_{LX}}{a_{KX}}(\overline{K} - K_Y) + \frac{a_{LY}}{a_{KY}} K_Y = \overline{L} \tag{9}$$

Since r_X is given by CRS, $\frac{a_{LX}}{a_{KX}}$ is given. Now as r_Y increases, from (2), $\frac{r_Y}{w}$ must rise and $\frac{a_{LY}}{a_{KY}}$ must rise as well. Hence in equation (9) the LHS unambiguously increases. To bring back the balance K_Y must fall substantially. As long as $\frac{a_{LY}}{a_{KY}} > \frac{a_{LX}}{a_{KX}}$, LHS must decrease with a decline in K_Y. Such an assumption implies that the informal sector is labor-intensive; an assumption by virtue of being realistic is kept all through the paper. Therefore as r_Y rises K_Y must fall. This defines *FF* in Figure (1). Once (r_Y, K_Y) are determined from Figure (1), the rest of the variables can be determined easily.

The key comparative static exercise we are interested in is a decline in '*t*'. Figure (1) helps us to trace out the consequences of both. A decline in *t* reduces r_X, given $\overline{w}$ and P_X. Given r_Y a drop in r_X increases K_Y, as $\phi' > 0$. This will mean a rightward shift of *MM* to $M'M'$.

At the same time given r_Y and K_Y, a drop in r_X reduces $\frac{a_{LX}}{a_{KX}}$ and therefore LHS in (9) declines. The balance is restored through an increase in K_Y at a given r_Y. *FF* shifts to the right as well. The way Figure (2) is drawn suggests that *Y* must expand. But r_Y may remain unchanged and can in fact go either way. Note that if *MM* shifts quite a bit relative to *FF*, r_Y will decline and w will increase. The mobility effect has to be significant for a positive effect on the informal wage. A drop in $\frac{a_{LX}}{a_{LY}}$ releases labor to *Y* sector, which implies that *FF* shifts up requiring more K_Y to accommodate displaced labor. Additional capital that comes to *Y* because is r_X lower must outweigh the required amount needed to absorb displaced labor at a given r_Y, hence at a given w to induce an increase in *w*.

With zero mobility *MM* is vertical and remain unchanged. Hence, r_Y must increase and w must decrease through a shift in *FF*. With perfect mobility *MM* is horizontal at $r_Y = r_X$ and as r_X drops, *MM* shifts down. Notwithstanding the shift in *FF*, r_Y must adjust to the new level of r_X and w must increase. Figure (3) describes the effects of such adjustments.

The above two cases explicitly demonstrate the *partial and general equilibrium* results that can be derived from this model. In figure 2, the vertical line MM represents perfect immobility of capital between the formal and the informal segments. Under the circumstances, formal job losses and crowding in of workers into the informal sector leads to wage cuts in the latter. The situation undergoes a complete reversal if capital is perfectly mobile and is represented by a horizontal line MM (figures 2 and 3). Retrenchments from the formal sector and additional job creation in the informal could even lead to a wage gain for the informal workers, thus establishing the general equilibrium implications of our model.

$$\hat{w} > 0, iff, \varepsilon > \sigma_X K_X f\left(\frac{\lambda_{LX}}{\lambda_{KX}}\right) \tag{10}$$

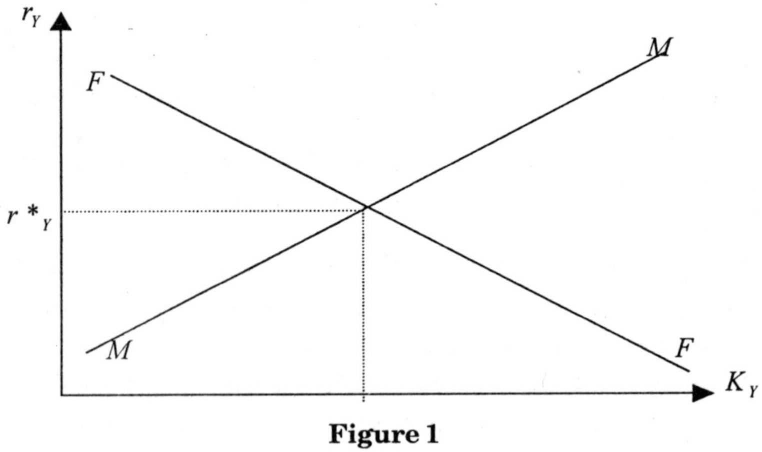

Figure 1

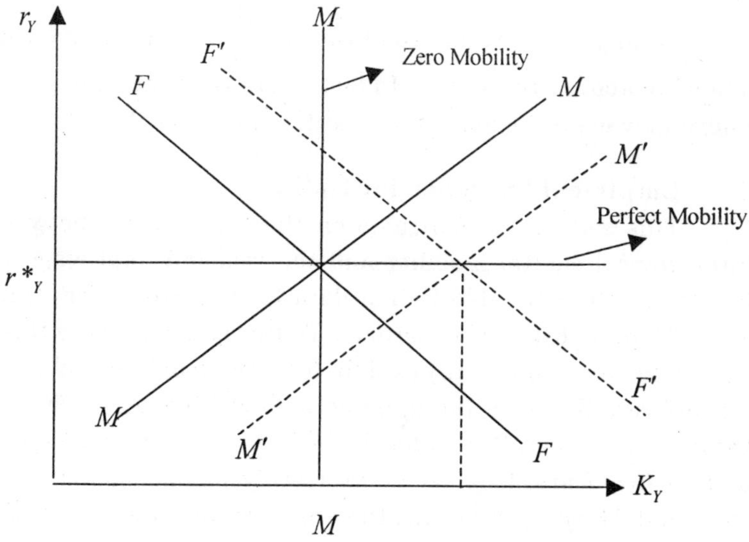

Figure 2

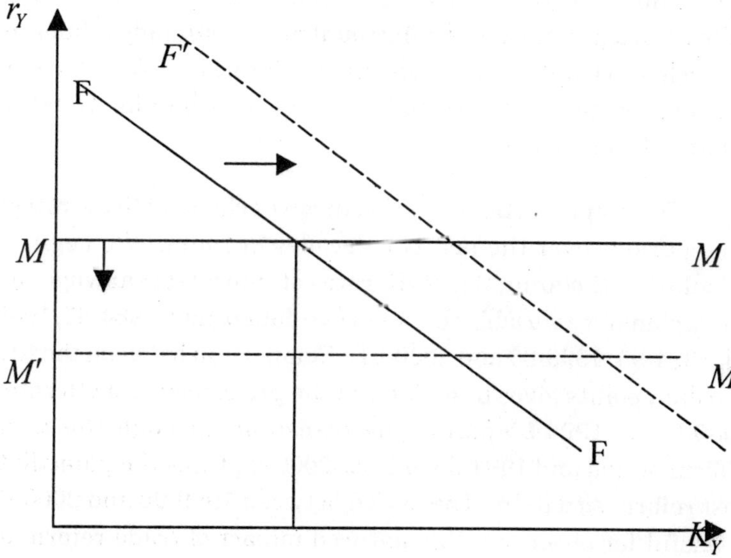

Figure 3

Finally, the precise condition for $\frac{dw}{dt} > 0$ is derived by following above arguments. In fact, there is an increase in the informal wage if the following condition is satisfied

4. Empirical Evidence for India

This section concentrates on the relationship between intersectoral capital mobility and the real informal wage by looking at the available Indian data for the pre-reform (pre-1991-92) and post-reform periods. To this end we choose three factors that can potentially explain the growth of informal wage for different states in India, namely, *Real Fixed Asset* (FA) in the informal sector, *Real Value Added* (VA) in the informal sector and the *Real Rural Wage* (RW). Previously, it has been discussed (Kar and Marjit, 2001) that the workers migrating from the rural areas cannot afford to wait indefinitely in the urban sector for a potential job opening, and instead join the urban informal sector for lower wages. When wages are high in the rural area they tend to migrate back. Informal employment and thus informal wage in the developing countries are strongly influenced by such seasonality of rural-urban migration. We therefore use rural wage as an exogenous variable in explaining trends in urban informal wage.

The empirical investigation involves choice of five strategic time periods over the last two decades in India. We begin by calculating the annual growth rates of informal real wage and the explanatory variables between five data points: 1984-85, 1989-90, 1994-95, 1999-00 and 2000-01.[4] Comparison between the first two data points gives us an idea on the pre-reform growth rates. 1989-90 to 1994-95 marks the transition through the trade reform period and 1994-95 to 1999-2000 captures the immediate post reform situation. The period between 1999-00 and 2000-01 is useful for observing the matured impact of trade reform on informal wage. Unavailability of a continuous time series restricts our choice to this five-point data set.

As already mentioned, we assume imperfect capital mobility between the formal and the informal sectors, which essentially means that following a contraction in the formal sector some capital may be relocated to the informal sector.[5] In our example, the capital reallocation occurs between the formal manufacturing sector and the non-directory manufacturing enterprises in the informal sector.[6] However, this is a proxy for measuring capital relocation between the sectors and we use the growth of real fixed assets in the informal sector as an explanatory factor for growth of the real informal wage. Finally, we use the real value added in the informal sector to see if that has sufficient explanatory power behind increases in the real informal wage. Obviously, the starting point of this analysis is the observation that the real informal wage has increased unambiguously in most states and union territories[7] in India, after the onset of trade liberalization. We provide this evidence in Table 1 (in Appendix II), initially for 15 major states and after 1989-90 for 30 states and union territories. Finally, we check for existence of structural breaks between the pre- and post-reform periods for the annual growth rates in informal wage.

Following the plan of empirical study, we begin by providing observations on the annual growth of real wage, real VA and real FA (in 1989 prices) for the informal sector as well as that of the real rural wage across different states and Union Territories in India. Due to incompleteness of the data, we calculate the real growth rates for only 17 states during 1984-85, and expand the set to include 30 states and union territories for 1989-90, 1994-95, 1999-2000 and 2000-01. Table 2 (Appendix II) offers detailed descriptive statistics for the variables under consideration and Table 3 shows that there does not exist any substantial problem of multi-collinearity among the variables.

The first of the three explanatory variables, *informal fixed assets* (real FA) grew at a temperate rate between 1984-85 and 1989-90 for many states (Fig. 5, Appendix II), although Assam

(AS), Haryana (HY), Kerala (KE), Tripura (TR) and West Bengal (WB) registered negative growth of informal real fixed assets during this period. However, during 1989-90 and 1994-95 immediately after the reforms took effect in India, informal fixed asset shows high growth rate in many of the states. Once again, Bihar (BH), Himachal Pradesh (HP), Lakshadweep (LA), Meghalaya (ME) etc., report negative growths. Between 1994-95 and 1999-2000 informal fixed assets grew positively (10% to 150%) for 29 out of 30 locations in India, with the exception of Manipur (MA). The pattern, however, seems dampened for many states during 1999-00 and 2000-01.

The second explanatory variable *real Value Added* (VA) also registered a negative trend for all states except Gujarat and West Bengal during 1984-85 and 1989-90. It undergoes a turn around in the post reform period, when most states and union territories show significant increase in the value added. Finally between 1999-00 and 2000-01 it reports negative growth rates in many states.[8]

Third, *real RW* denotes the real growth rate of rural wage. It shows negative growth rates for all the states between 1984-85 and 1989-90, which changes to positive growth rates between 1989-90 and 1994-95 for majority of the states. However, this was not sustained, since between 1994-95 and 1999-00 relatively more states like TR, Andaman and Nicobar Islands (AN), SI, Jammu and Kashmir (JK) etc., once again record negative growth in rural wage, which continues to later periods.

The dependent variable in our model, the growth rate of *real informal wage* (IW) shows a negative growth for all the states between 1984-85 and 1989-90 (see Figure 4 and Table 1). The trend shifted substantially in favor of informal workers in the period immediately following the introduction of economic reforms in India. All the states including, GJ, MH, OR (22%), TN, RJ (32%), AP (38%) showed significant positive annual growth in informal wages. Between 1994-95 and 1999-00, twenty-nine out of thirty locations, except WB (-2%) show moderate positive annual growth of informal wage and the post reform average annual growth in informal wage is recorded at between 15-20% with a variance of 26% between states.

Based on these observations, we offer results from a generalized least square regression (Table 4), where real informal wage is regressed on real FA, real VA and real RW after correcting for presence of heteroscedasticity in the error terms. Between 1984-85 and 1989-90 (denoted as 1989-90 in Table 4), all the elements significantly explain changes in the informal real wage. Notably, the intercept term is negative. Admittedly, the explanatory power of the regression (Adjusted R-squares) analysis declines over time and it is lowest for the growth rates between 1994-95 and 1999-00 with the consequence that real VA alone is capable of explaining positively and significantly the growth in real informal wage. One can nevertheless, observe from this cross-section that the informal wage has experienced shifts in both direction and magnitude between pre-reform and post-reform periods as have been the factors deemed most responsible for its movements. For example, the growth in real rural wage affects the real informal wage negatively (and significantly) in the last period, unlike in the first three.

Subsequently, we offer a pooled (a pseudo panel) regression for these variables and report the findings in Table 5. The panel regression initially tests for whether the fixed effects (FE) or the random effects (RE) model is consistent with the data, given that the FE/RE is the natural choice over classical regression (CR) model since the value of Lagrange Multiplier is very large. Further, between FE and RE the results from the Hausman Test suggests that FE is the appropriate model to use. Consequently, we use the methodology of Least Squares

Dummy Variables after correcting for heteroscedasticity.[9] According to this model, however, the Real FA and real RW are not significant, although, the former shows a positive impact on real IW. Real VA on the other hand is positive and highly significant (at 1% level) in explaining the increase in real IW. The added information that this exercise offers is that, despite shifting importance attached to real FA and real VA in explaining real IW as witnessed from the cross-section regression results, the general trend seems to be that both real FA and real VA can explain growth in real IW positively. However, it also appears that the negative impact of the rural wage as observed during the last growth phase dominates the general trend.

Finally we offer results from the investigation into the existence of structural breaks in the real IW. To this extent, we use the standard Chow test and identify that there exists multiple structural breaks over the entire span of the period, including 1994-95, 1999-00 and 2000-01 as the break years. Table 6 indicates that both the intercept and the slope have changed significantly over time. The graphical representation of the nature of the changes in the Annual Informal Wage Growth is given in Figure 7. The graphical representation clearly shows the jumps and changes in both intercepts and slopes as we have discussed above.

5. Concluding Remarks

The purpose of this paper has been to look into the impact of trade reform policies on informal wage in a typical developing economy. The fact that poor informal workers must find employment for survival, allows us to use a full-employment model in a general equilibrium setting. By using a generalized theoretical construct we have proposed and demonstrated that a crucial factor, which determines the wage-employment status of the existing informal workers, is the degree of capital mobility between the formal and the informal sectors. As formal sector contracts due to tariff liberalization and retrenched workers crowd into the informal sector for employment, informal wage does not necessarily fall. If capital also starts moving out into the informal sector, it is quite likely that informal wage will rise provided the degree of capital mobility is not very low. This tends to criticize the argument that more employment in the informal sector signifies lower wage for the average informal worker. We have characterized the cases with perfect and zero mobility of capital demonstrating two extreme situations. Modeling the degree of capital mobility explicitly in an otherwise simple general equilibrium structure clearly establishes the result.

The empirical section is however, not a direct test of the theoretical results for reasons mentioned above. Instead, we use data from the informal sector in India to reflect on the testable hypothesis in an exploratory sense. The informal sector in India has registered an annual increase in the real wages by 15-20% during the post-reform decade. At the same time, there have been substantial increments in the real fixed assets and real value added in the sector. We show that both these factors, as also the real rural wage in the country explain growth in the real informal wage positively and significantly for most of the time periods under consideration. The accumulation of real fixed assets in the informal sector corresponds with declining real capital stock in the formal sector, which in our case exemplifies the issue of capital mobility discussed above. Interestingly, the growth of fixed assets in the informal sector convincingly outweighs the growth of fixed capital stock in the organized sector in the post-reform phase. In the absence of data on the path that each unit of capital follows as and when relocated, this is used as a proxy measure.

The message that this study intends to drive in is simple and clear. If one has to study the impact of reform on labor markets, one has to look at the working of the capital market as well. While greater employment in the informal sector can be a sign of both poverty and prosperity, the true outcomes are distinctly visible only when the role of the capital market is also taken into consideration. To make the problem a meaningful exercise, we checked whether a substantial rise in capital stock in informal manufacturing is consistent with a phase of either a meager or a negative growth of fixed capital stock in the organized manufacturing.

As an extension one could bring agriculture into the picture with mobile labor and fixed supply of land. It is also possible to show how profitability in agriculture can influence the informal wage with or without capital mobility, an exercise undoubtedly relevant for the developing economies. Thus, the analysis should also be useful for cross-country empirical studies in future. We have kept the commodity prices fixed by the small country assumption. Alternatively, one can introduce a homothetic demand function and with the elasticity of substitution in demand crossing a critical threshold, all our results will hold. One may argue that we have ignored the 'non-traded' characteristic of the informal sector. However, it follows from our basic model that bringing in a second informal sector producing a non-traded good does not add much to the results. If capital is highly mobile, tariff reform must increase the informal wage and reduce the return to capital. The price of the non-traded good can move in any direction. Finally, the impact on the informal wage should remain the same, qualitatively.

References

Agenor, P., 1996, The labor market and economic adjustment, IMF Staff Papers 32, 261-335.

Agenor, P & P. Montiel, 1996, Development Macroeconomics, Princeton, NJ: Princeton University Press.

Basu, Kaushik, 1984, The Less Developed Economy – A Critique of

Contemporary Theory; Delhi: Oxford University Press.

Carruth, A & A. Oswald, 1981, The determination of union and non-union wage rates, European Economic Review 16, 2/3, 285-302.

Davis, Lewis S., 2006, Growing apart: The division of labor and the breakdown of informal institutions, Journal of Comparative Economics, 34, 1, 75–91.

De Soto, Hernando., 2000, The Mystery of Capital, USA: Basic Books.

Fields, G., 1975, Rural urban migration, urban employment and job search activity in less developed countries, Journal of Development Economics, 2, 165–188.

Gang, Ira N. and Shubhashis Gangopadhyay, 1990, A model of the informal sector in development, Journal of Economic Studies, 17, 5, 19-32.

Gupta, M. R., 1993, Rural urban migration, informal sector and development policies — a theoretical analysis, Journal of Development Economics, 41, 137–151.

Gupta, M. R., 1997, Informal sector and informal capital market in a small open less developed economy, Journal of Development Economics, 52, 409–428.

Greene, William, 2003, Econometric Analysis, New York: Prentice Hall, 5th Edition.

International Labour Organisation (ILO), 1999, Key indicators of the labour market. Geneva: International Labour Office.

ILO, 1972, Employment, Incomes and Equality: A Strategy for Increasing Productive Employment in Kenya. Geneva: ILO.

Kar, S & Sugata Marjit, 2001, Informal sector in general equilibrium: welfare effects of trade policy reforms, International Review of Economics and Finance 10, 289-300.

LIMDEP 7.0 by William Greene.

Mazumdar, Dipak, 1976, The rural-urban wage-gap, migration and the shadow wage, Oxford Economic Papers, 28,3, 406-425.

Mazumdar, Dipak, 1983, Segmented labor markets in LDCs, American Economic Review, 73, 2, 254-59.

Marjit, Sugata, 2003, Economic reform and informal wage- A general equilibrium analysis, Journal of Development Economics, 72, 371-378.

Marjit, S & H. Beladi, 2002, The Stolper-Samuelson theorem in a wage differential framework, The Japanese Economic Review 53, 2, 177-181.

NSSO, Survey of Unorganized Manufacturing Sector in India, Department of Statistics and Programme Implementation, Government of India - various issues.

Turnham, D., 1993, *Employment and Development — A New Review of Evidence*. Paris: Development Centre Studies, OECD.

Webster, L., & Fidler, P., 1996, The Informal Sector and Microfinance in West Africa. Washington, DC: World Bank Regional and Sectoral Studies, World Bank.

Appendix I

Proof of condition (10)

$$\overline{w}a_{LX} + r_X a_{KX} = P_X(1+t) \quad \textbf{(A.1)}$$

$$wa_{LY} + r_Y a_{KY} = P_Y \quad \textbf{(A.2)}$$

$$\frac{K_X}{K_Y} = \phi\left(\frac{r_X}{r_Y}\right), \phi' > 0$$

$$\frac{\overline{K} - K_Y}{K_Y} = \phi\left(\frac{r_X}{r_Y}\right) \quad \textbf{(A.3)}$$

From (A.1), $\hat{r}_X \theta_{KX} = \hat{P}_X - \theta_{LX}\hat{\overline{w}}$

$$= \hat{P}_X(1 - \theta_{LX}\alpha) \quad \textbf{(A.4)}$$

Where, $\hat{\overline{w}} = \alpha\hat{P}_X + \beta\hat{P}_Y = \alpha\hat{P}_X$, since, $\hat{P}_Y = 0$.

From (A.2), $\hat{w}\theta_{LY} + \hat{r}_Y\theta_{KY} = 0$. This implies, $\hat{w} = -\frac{\theta_{KY}}{\theta_{LY}}\hat{r}_Y$. **(A.5)**

Now using equations (3) to (6),

$$a_{LX}X + a_{LY}Y = \overline{L}$$

Reformulating, $\frac{a_{LX}}{a_{KX}}(\overline{K} - K_Y) + \frac{a_{LY}}{a_{KY}}K_Y = \overline{L}$

Again, $\lambda_{LX}\hat{X} + \lambda_{LY}\hat{Y} + \lambda_{LX}\hat{a}_{LX} + \lambda_{LY}\hat{a}_{LY} = 0$

And $\lambda_{LX}\hat{K}_X + \lambda_{LY}\hat{K}_Y + \lambda_{LX}(\hat{a}_{LX} - \hat{a}_{KX})$

$$+ \lambda_{LY}(\hat{a}_{LY} - \hat{a}_{KY}) = 0 \quad \textbf{(A.6)}$$

But, as $K_X = \overline{K} - K_Y$

$\hat{K}_X = -\hat{K}_Y / \phi$, where $\phi = (K_X / K_Y)$.

Substituting these information in (A.6),

$$-\frac{1}{\phi}\lambda_{LX}\hat{K}_Y+\lambda_{LY}\hat{K}_Y+\lambda_{LX}\sigma_X\hat{r}_X-\lambda_{LY}\sigma_Y(\hat{w}-\hat{r}_Y)=0 \quad \textbf{(A.7)}$$

Rearranging, and using (A.4), and $\theta_{LY}(\hat{w}-\hat{r})=-\hat{r}_Y$

$$(\lambda_{LY}-\frac{1}{\phi}\lambda_{LX})\hat{K}_Y+\lambda_{LX}\sigma_X\hat{P}_X\left(\frac{1-\theta_{LX}\alpha}{\theta_{KX}}\right)+\lambda_{LY}\sigma_Y\frac{\hat{r}_Y}{\theta_{LY}}=0$$

Thus, $$(\lambda_{LY}-\frac{1}{\phi}\lambda_{LX})\hat{K}_Y+\sigma_Y\frac{\lambda_{LY}}{\theta_{LY}}\hat{r}_Y=-\lambda_{LX}\sigma_X\hat{P}_X\left(\frac{1-\theta_{LX}\alpha}{\theta_{KX}}\right) \quad \textbf{(A.8)}$$

Now, taking '*ln*' on (A.3),

$\ln(\overline{K}-K_Y)-\ln K_Y=\ln\phi\left(\frac{r_X}{r_Y}\right)$. Taking percentage changes,

$$\hat{K}_X-\hat{K}_Y=\frac{1}{\phi}d\phi=\frac{1}{\phi}\frac{\delta\phi}{\delta\left(\frac{r_X}{r_Y}\right)}\frac{r_Ydr_X-r_Xdr_Y}{r_Y^2}$$

$$=\frac{\phi'}{\phi}\frac{r_X}{r_Y}(\hat{r}_X-\hat{r}_Y)$$

Using (A.4),

or, $$\hat{K}_X-\hat{K}_Y+\frac{\phi'}{\phi}\frac{r_X}{r_Y}\hat{r}_Y=\frac{\phi'}{\phi}\frac{r_X}{r_Y}[\hat{P}_X(1-\theta_{LX}\alpha)/\theta_{KX}]$$

We define, $\varepsilon=\frac{\delta\phi}{\delta(r_X/r_Y)}\frac{r_X/r_Y}{\phi}$, as the elasticity of capital mobility between sectors X and Y.

Thus, $$-\hat{K}_Y[1+\frac{1}{\phi}]+\varepsilon.\hat{r}_Y=\varepsilon\hat{P}_X(1-\theta_{LX}\alpha)$$

Therefore, $$\hat{r}_Y=\hat{K}_Y\frac{1}{\varepsilon}[1+\frac{1}{\phi}]+\hat{P}_X(1-\theta_{LX}\alpha) \quad \textbf{(A.9)}$$

Rearranging equations (A.6) and (A.7),

Define, $$\mu=(\lambda_{LY}-\frac{1}{\phi}\lambda_{LX})=\left(\frac{\lambda_{LY}}{\lambda_{KY}}-\frac{\lambda_{LX}}{\lambda_{KX}}\right)K_X$$

$$= \frac{\lambda_{LX}}{\lambda_{KX}} \frac{K_X}{\left(\frac{\lambda_{LY}}{\lambda_{KY}} - \frac{\lambda_{LX}}{\lambda_{KX}}\right)} \qquad \textbf{(A.10)}$$

$$\sigma_Y \frac{\lambda_{LY}}{\theta_{LY}} \hat{r}_Y + \mu \hat{K}_Y = -\lambda_{LX}\sigma_X \hat{P}_X \left(\frac{1-\theta_{LX}\alpha}{\theta_{KX}}\right) \qquad \textbf{(A.11)}$$

and

$$\hat{r}_Y - \frac{(\phi+1)}{\phi\varepsilon}\hat{K}_Y = \hat{P}_X(1-\theta_{LX}\alpha) \qquad \textbf{(A.12)}$$

Using Cramer's rule to solve for $\hat{r}_Y$.

$$D = \begin{bmatrix} (\sigma_Y \frac{\lambda_{LY}}{\theta_{LY}} + \frac{\lambda_{LZ}}{\theta_{TZ}} \frac{\theta_{KY}}{\theta_{LY}} \sigma_Z) & \mu \\ 1 & -\frac{(\phi+1)}{\phi\varepsilon} \end{bmatrix} = \begin{bmatrix} -\frac{\sigma_Y \frac{\lambda_{LY}}{\theta_{LY}}(\phi+1)}{\phi\varepsilon} - \mu \end{bmatrix} < 0$$

Therefore, $\hat{r}_Y = \frac{1}{D}[\frac{\lambda_{LX}\sigma_X \alpha(\phi+1)}{\phi\varepsilon} - \mu]\hat{P}_X(1-\theta_{LX}\alpha)$ **(A.13)**

Now, suppose $\hat{P}_X < 0$, then $\hat{r}_Y > 0$ iff, $\frac{\lambda_{LX}\sigma_X(\phi+1)}{\phi\varepsilon} > \mu$

Finally, using (A.5)

$$\hat{w} > 0, \text{ iff, } \frac{\lambda_{LX}\sigma_X(\phi+1)}{\phi} < \mu\varepsilon \qquad \textbf{(A.14)}$$

or, $\varepsilon > \frac{\lambda_{LX}\sigma_X(\phi+1)}{\phi\mu}$

or, $\varepsilon > \frac{\lambda_{LX}\sigma_X}{\mu}\frac{\phi+1}{\phi} = \frac{\lambda_{LX}\sigma_X}{\mu}\frac{1+\frac{K_X}{K_Y}}{\frac{K_X}{K_Y}} = \frac{\lambda_{LX}\sigma_X}{\mu}\frac{\bar{K}}{K_Y}\frac{K_Y}{K_X} = \frac{\lambda_{LX}}{\lambda_{KX}}\frac{\sigma_X}{\mu}$

Using (A.8), $\hat{w} > 0$, iff, $\varepsilon > \sigma_X K_X f\left(\frac{\lambda_{LX}}{\lambda_{KX}}\right)$

The above derivation provides the proof of condition (10).

Appendix II
Annual Growth Rate of Informal Real Wage

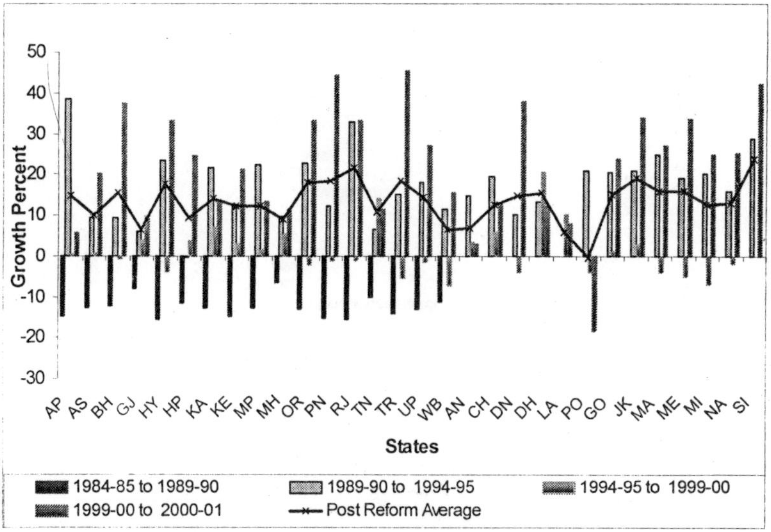

Source: NSS Reports, various rounds and own calculations.

Figure 4
List of Abbreviations for States and Union Territories in India

AP – Andhra Pradesh, AS – Assam, BH – Bihar, GJ – Gujarat, HY – Haryana

HP – Himachal Pradesh, KA – Karnataka, KE – Kerala, MP – Madhya Pradesh

MH – Maharashtra, OR – Orissa, PN – Punjab, RJ – Rajasthan, TN – Tamil Nadu

TR – Tripura, UP – Uttar Pradesh, WB – West Bengal, AN – Andaman and Nicobar Islands

Ch – Chandigarh, DN – Dadra and Nagar Haveli, DH – Delhi, LA – Lakshadweep

PO – Pondicherry, GO – Goa, JK – Jammu and Kashmir, MA – Manipur

ME – Meghalaya, MI – Mizoram, NA – Nagaland, SI - Sikkim.

Figure 5

Annual Growth Rates for Formal Real Capital Stock and Informal Real Fixed Asset

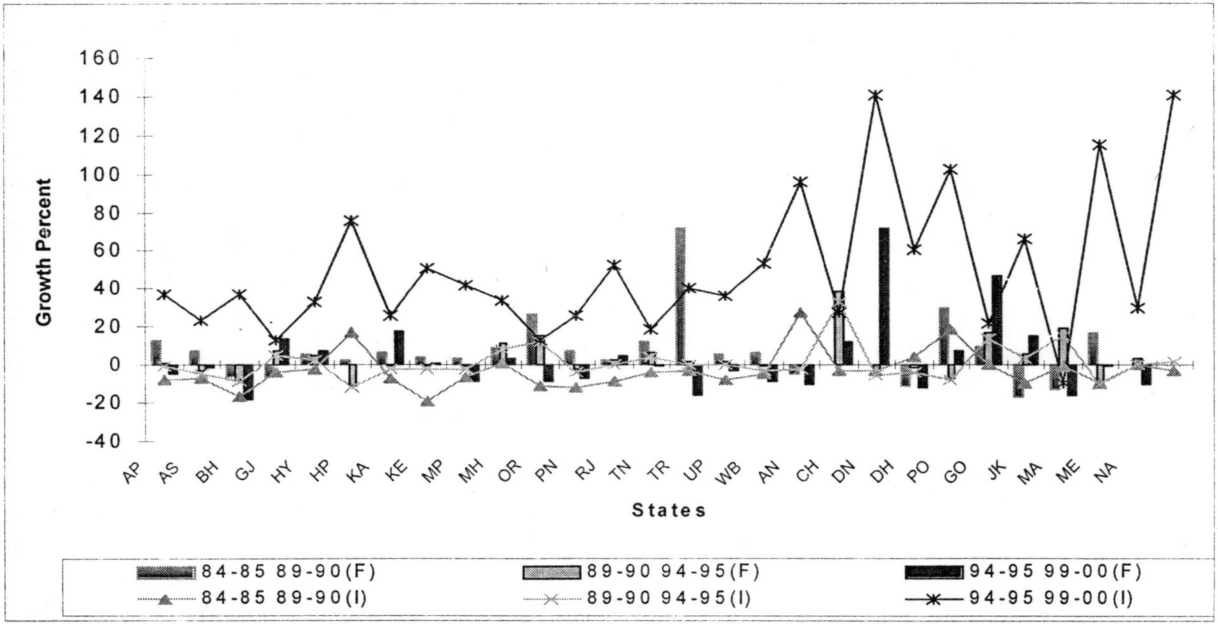

F – Formal Sector, I – Informal Sector.

Source: NSS Various rounds, ASI Reports, GOI and own calculations.

Figure-6

Annual Growth Rate of Informal Wage between 1984-85 and 2000-01

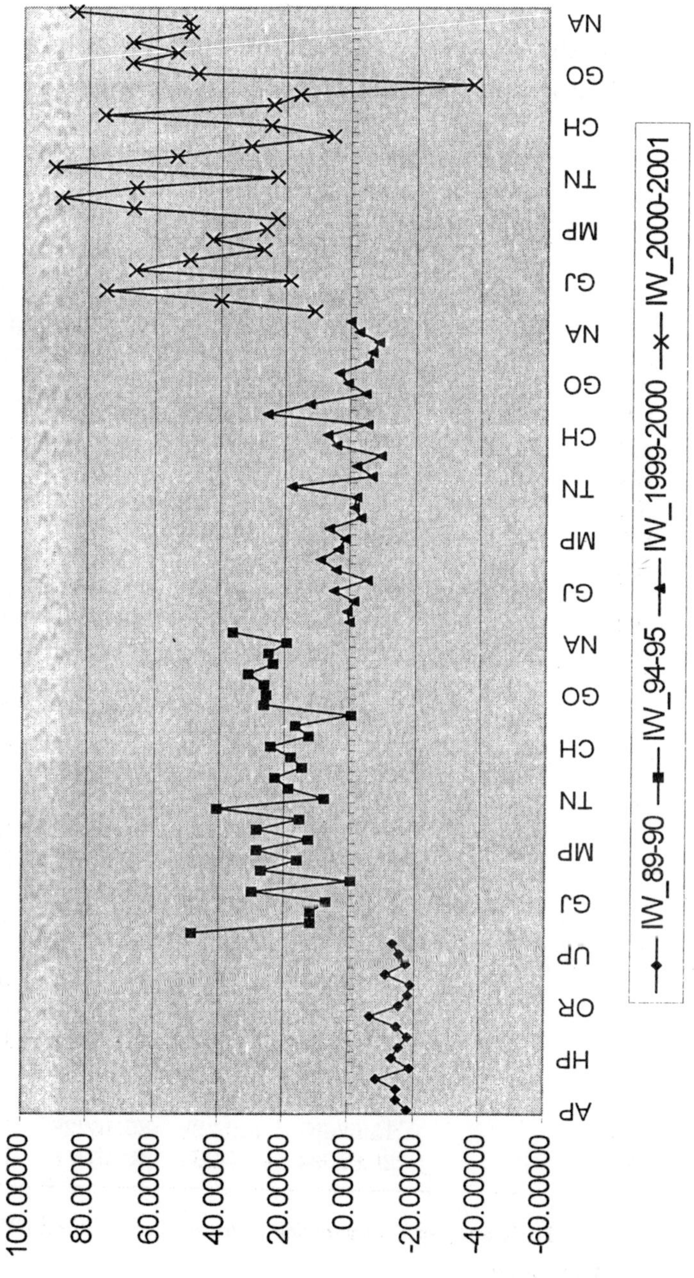

Table 1

Table Showing Annual Growth Rates of Real Informal Wage for States and Union Territories in India

States	*1984-85 to 1989-90*	*1989-90 to 1994-95*	*1994-95 to 1999-00*	*1999-00 to 2000-01*	*Post Reform Average*
AP	-14.9383	38.37914	0.351421	5.54216	14.75757
AS	-12.5909	9.400387	0.502013	19.94701	9.949804
BH	-12.4796	9.259229	-0.91022	37.41843	15.25582
GJ	-8.01461	5.856186	3.761828	9.471879	6.363298
HY	-15.417	23.39205	-4.11872	33.07289	17.44874
HP	-11.5206	-0.34082	3.509483	24.55454	9.241068
KA	-12.8237	21.54953	7.021524	13.43834	14.00313
KE	-14.8953	12.55645	2.686628	21.20452	12.1492
MP	-12.6123	22.41174	1.455013	13.11878	12.32851
MH	-6.4	9.7482	5.247609	11.28708	8.760962
OR	-13.1553	22.78583	-2.38878	33.1919	17.86298
PN	-15.1443	12.20414	-1.06954	44.061	18.39853
RJ	-15.4959	32.53101	-1.34439	33.03571	21.40744
TN	-10.1074	6.406688	14.13201	11.49062	10.67644
TR	-14.3066	14.89337	-5.45877	45.36927	18.26796
UP	-13.2014	18.00436	-1.58454	26.79013	14.40332
WB	-11.2556	11.41085	-7.25447	15.29931	6.485231
AN		14.62978	3.202789	2.910365	6.914311
CH		19.21098	5.496664	12.4677	12.39178
DN		9.828439	-4.01589	37.7676	14.52672
DH		13.26679	20.39249	12.10498	15.25476
LA		-0.21334	9.929694	7.832409	5.849589
PO		20.77112	-3.96475	-18.5548	-0.58281
GO		20.50309	0.947838	23.74566	15.06553
JK		20.71262	2.838103	33.64066	19.06379
MA		24.9116	-4.18481	26.83254	15.85311
ME		18.91503	-5.28746	33.57459	15.73405
MI		19.93168	-6.92451	24.69716	12.56811
NA		15.62657	-1.96228	25.16228	12.94219
SI		28.81384	-0.01264	42.15758	23.65293

Source: NSS Reports on Unorganized Sector in India, Various Rounds, and Own Calculations.

Table 2. Descriptive Statistics for the Variables (Year-Wise)

Year	*Variables*	*Mean*	*SD*	*Skewness*	*Kurtosis*	*Minimum*	*Maximum*	*Observations*
1989-90	IW	(-) 15.08	3.45	0.97	3.16	(-) 18.96	(-) 6.75	17
	FA	4.71	9.29	0.54	3.18	(-) 10.75	26.92	17
	VA	(-) 7.90	7.12	1.20	4.20	(-) 19.04	10.00	17
	RW	(-) 7.56	3.48	(-) 0.13	1.94	(-) 14.38	(-) 2.80	17
1994-95	IW	20.72	10.97	0.22	3.03	(-) 0.43	47.97	30
	FA	3.23	12.93	1.36	5.99	(-) 19.28	47.98	30
	VA	5.89	13.31	1.98	7.94	(-) 12.24	56.44	30
	RW	8.03	6.94	(-) 0.37	2.90	(-) 8.23	20.73	28
1999-2000	IW	1.29	7.65	1.26	4.76	(-) 9.07	25.49	30
	FA	58.50	50.32	1.35	4.16	(-) 13.24	208.01	30
	VA	42.05	32.67	1.47	4.93	3.48	140.38	30
	RW	5.91	13.94	0.08	2.71	(-) 25.00	37.93	30

(Contd.)

(Contd. Table 2)

Year	*Variables*	*Mean*	*SD*	*Skewness*	*Kurtosis*	*Minimum*	*Maximum*	*Observations*
2000-2001	IW	44.18	28.51	(-) 0.52	3.30	(-) 37.11	90.74	30
	FA	(-) 10.52	35.77	0.87	4.19	(-) 69.15	99.74	30
	VA	(-) 40.18	25.04	0.82	4.42	(-) 94.69	26.49	30
	RW	(-) 2.07	17.17	2.22	7.34	(-) 19.91	58.87	29
All years	IW	16.16	26.84	0.81	3.20	(-) 37.11	90.74	107
	FA	15.10	43.33	1.69	7.54	(-) 69.15	208.01	107
	VA	0.92	38.68	0.59	4.54	(-) 94.69	140.38	107
	RW	2.13	13.52	1.12	5.14	(-) 25.00	58.87	104

Description of the variables:

IW = Annual Growth rate of real informal wage
FA = Annual Growth rate of real fixed assets
VA = Annual Growth rate of real value-added
RW = Annual Growth rate of real rural wage

Table 3. Correlation Coefficient Matrix (Year-Wise)

1989-90	*IW*	*FA*	*VA*	*RW*
IW	1.00000	.42767	.57368	.27155
FA	.42767	1.00000	.37750	-.09812
VA	.57368	.37750	1.00000	-.03692
RW	.27155	-.09812	-.03692	1.00000
1994-95	IW	FA	VA	RW
IW	1.00000	.33932	.27046	.28607
FA	.33932	1.00000	.04867	.00108
VA	.27046	.04867	1.00000	.17476
RW	.28607	.00108	.17476	1.00000
1999-2000	IW	FA	VA	RW
IW	1.00000	.06356	.35441	.14441
FA	.06356	1.00000	.13441	-.38761
VA	.35441	.13441	1.00000	-.07614
RW	.14441	-.38761	-.07614	1.00000
2000-2001	IW	FA	VA	RW
IW	1.00000	.15125	.54512	-.15355
FA	.15125	1.00000	-.20262	.16064
VA	.54512	-.20262	1.00000	.02964
RW	-.15355	.16064	.02964	1.00000

Table 4. Regression Results for Individual Time-Points Corrected for Heteroscadasticity

METHODOLOGY: Generalized Least Squares
Dependent variable: Annual Growth Rate of IW

Year	*Exp. Variables*	*Coeff.*	*t-ratio*	R^2	*Adj.* R^2	*AIC*	*LL*
1989-90	CONSTANT	(-) 11.35	(-) 6.70473*	0.48	0.36	5.01	(-) 39.10
	FA	0.102	2.58869*				
	VA	0.233	5.09886*				
	RW	0.313	1.73243**				
1994-95	CONSTANT	15.89	8.84668*	0.23	0.14	7.59	(-) 109.98
	FA	0.278	2.19006*				
	VA	0.183	1.74465**				
	RW	0.354	1.89854**				

(Contd.)

(Contd.Table 4)

Year	*Exp. Variables*	*Coeff.*	*t-ratio*	R^2	*Adj.* R^2	*AIC*	*LL*
1999-2000	CONSTANT	(-) 3.76	(-) 1.62243	0.16	0.06	6.961	(-) 100.42
	FA	0.014	0.45872				
	VA	0.083	2.04059**				
	RW	0.114	0.98769				
2000-2001	CONSTANT	69.56	5.69114*	0.30	0.23	9.41	(-) 137.09
	FA	0.152	0.86366				
	VA	0.607	2.23908*				
	RW	(-) 0.307	(-) 2.30538*				

Note: * denotes significance at 5% level; ** denotes significance at 10% level
Adj. R^2 = adjusted R^2
AIC = Akaike Information Criterion
LL = Log-likelihood

Table 5. Unbalanced Panel Regression

Random Effects Model: v(i, t) = e(i, t) + u(i) Methodology: 2-step GLS

| Estimates: Var [e] = 0.251075D+03

| Var [u] = 0.145978D+04

| Corr [v(i, t),v(i, s)] = 0.853246

| **Lagrange Multiplier Test vs. Model (3) = 157.18 (1 df, prob value = 0.000000)**

| (High values of LM favor FEM/REM over CR model.)

| **Fixed vs. Random Effects (Hausman) = 2.07 (3 df, prob value = 0 .558458)**

| (High (low) values of H favor FEM (REM).)

| Reestimated using GLS coefficients:

| Estimates: Var[e] = 0.251113D+03

| Var[u] = 0.304627D+04

| Sum of Squares = 0.106765D+06

| R-squared = -0.398626D+00

RE model is inconsistent, which leads us to use a Fixed Effects Model. The results from the LSDV (Group Dummy) model is given below.

Least Squares with Group Dummy Variables

| Ordinary least squares regression Weighting variable = none

| **Dependent variable = REALIW** Mean= 16.16169250, S.D.= 26.83556242

| Model size: Observations = 107, Parameters = 7, Deg. Fr.= 100

| Residuals: Sum of squares= 25107.46507, Std. Dev = 15.84534

| **Fit: R-squared= .671091, Adjusted R-squared = .65136**

| Model test: **F [6, 100] = 34.01**, Probability value = 0.00000

| Diagnostic: **Log-L = -443.8343**, Restricted (b=0) Log-L = -503.3250

| Log Amemiya Probability Criterion. = 5.589, **Akaike Info. Criterion = 8.427**

| Estd. Autocorrelation of e (i, t) .139228 **White/Hetero-scedasticity corrected covariance matrix used.**

Results from Heteroscedasticty-corrected Panel (Fixed Effects) Regression

Explanatory Variable	*Coefficient*	*Standard Error*	*t-ratio*
REALFA	0.030422	0.049421	0.616
REALVA	0.256675**	0.070371	3.647
REALRW	-0.04538	0.160961	-0.282

** Significant at 5% level

Table 6. Identifying Structural Breaks

Years	*Exp. Variables*	*Coeff.*	*t-ratio*
1989-90 & 1994-95	FA	(-) 0.03	(-) 0.13698
Checking for structural breaks at 1994-95	VA	0.546	1.85573
	RW	1.22	2.92752
T2 = INTERCEPT DUMMY	T2	16.00	4.26033*
FA2 = T2 INTERACTS WITH FA	FA2	0.396	1.05172
VA2 = T2 INTERACTS WITH VA	VA2	0.064	0.154686
RW2 = T2 INTERACTS WITH RW	RW2	(-) 1.04	(-) 1.8349
1994-95 & 1999-2000	FA	0.307	2.41241
Checking for structural breaks at 1999-00	VA	0.309	1.91503
	RW	1.41	6.34088
T3 = INTERCEPT DUMMY	T3	(-) 3.76	(-) 0.81685
FA3 = T3 INTERACTS WITH FA	FA3	(-) 0.383	(-) 2.23524*
VA3 = T3 INTERACTS WITH VA	VA3	(-) 0.226	(-) 1.29278
RW3 = T3 INTERACTS WITH RW	RW3	(-) 1.29	(-) 4.64913*

(Contd.)

(Contd. Table 6)

Years	*Exp. Variables*	*Coeff.*	*t-ratio*
1999-2000 & 2000-2001	FA	(-) 0.008	(-) 0.14337
Checking for structural breaks at 2000-01	VA	0.054	0.611483
	RW	0.052	0.220547
T4 = INTERCEPT DUMMY	T4	69.56	10.3654*
FA4 = T4 INTERACTS WITH FA	FA4	0.160	1.4042
VA4 = T4INTERACTS WITH VA	VA4	0.553	3.37302*
RW4 = T4 INTERACTS WITH RW	RW4	(-) 0.359	(-) 1.15813

Dependent variable = Annual Growth Rate of IW

References

1. Earlier, De Soto (1989) pointed out that a heavy burden of taxes, bribes and inflexible bureaucratic regulations in the formal sector drives many producers into the informal sector; and similar arguments in Gang and Gangopadhyay (1990).
2. See Appendix I for detailed algebraic proof.
3. Condition (10) offers a directly testable hypothesis. However, it requires matching data on product specific capital stock in both formal and informal sectors, and the return such capital fetches in each sector. Annual Survey of Industries in India offer data on formal commodities until 1997 only, and reliable data on the return to capital in the informal sector is unavailable. Thus, we set aside this direct exercise for a future effort and instead use a proxy measure presently.
4. Secondary data on Informal sector activities in India is available from intermittent (usually every five year) sample surveys by NSSO (National Sample Survey Organization), Govt. of India.
5. Interest rate cuts in the commercial banks along with high volatility and lack of trust on the functioning of the stock exchanges might have contributed substantially to such capital flight for supporting informal activities. While this requires

further evidence and more detailed analysis, it is also believed that a large section of the retrenched labor has used their early retirement benefits and severance pays as startup capital for small businesses. Undoubtedly further research is needed to track the relocation path for such capital stock deterministically.

6. This is not to preclude the possibility that formal industrial capital may relocate to say, services within the formal sector. Howeve-, the overwhelming fixed assets formation in the informal sector along with falling capital stock in the formal suggests that a large portion of the investments previously in the formal sector has flown in to the informal segment, especially when the total savings in India has not changed significantly.
7. Regions directly administered by the central government.
8. Data and trends for this variable are available on request. We do not explicitly report them here.
9. See Greene (2003) for details on the methodology.

3

Lessons from the Lewis Model: Is growth sustainable?[1]

Amitava Bose

In the wake of India achieving high rates of growth of real GDP per capita, the question is: will these last? The answer to this question depends on the model of long-run growth that best fits India.

The idea that India has vast reserves of labour waiting to be usefully employed looks like a wonderfully attractive economic advantage. The model that best captures this kind of advantage is the Lewis model of growth, a model that every development economics text book has exploited. The lessons from that model, including those that may not apply, are worth considering.

1. Introductory Remarks on the Lewis Model

The Lewis model consists of a 'backward sector' B and an 'advanced sector' A. The latter requires labour and the former supplies it. The central assumption of the model is that increases in the demand for labour do not raise real wages[2]. This assumption – called the assumption of 'unlimited supplies of labour' – is captured in terms of a horizontal supply curve of labour. Such a supply curve can be explained in different ways (Lewis, 1954; Sen, 1966; Basu, 1984; Ray, 1998). Generally speaking the horizontal supply curve has been linked to the existence of 'surplus labour' in the backward sector. In what follows the terms 'unlimited supplies of labour', 'surplus labour', and 'horizontal supply curve' are used interchangeably because the focus of the paper is on the macroeconomic conclusions of the model and not on the microeconomic foundations. All we need to say is this: A is best seen as a 'small country' (referring to the practice in trade theory) or a 'price taker' (referring to the practice in microeconomic theory) with a demand that contributes insignificantly to the economy's overall demand for unskilled labour.[3]

The chief conclusion of the Lewis model is that surplus labour in B is a necessary condition for sustained growth in A. To see this we set out an extended version of the Lewis in which the supply curve is redrawn to allow also for the possibility that surplus labour is exhausted. Moreover, labour supply is affected by population growth in B. Different outcomes for long run equilibrium – or steady state – are possible in the extended Lewis model and it is useful to distinguish between these.

The analysis of growth possibilities leads to practical questions of importance. After setting out the extended Lewis model, we discuss some questions that are left open for future work.

2. The Lewis Model: An Extended Version

The model consists of two sectors. The 'advanced' sector (A) knows how to use capital goods and how to produce additional capital goods. It needs to import labour from elsewhere for production. The 'backward' sector (B) uses labour (surplus) and land (scarce and non-reproducible) to produce consumable output.

The central assumption of the original Lewis model is the continuing unlimited availability of labour from B to A at a constant minimum wage $\bar{w}$ (see Fig.1 below).

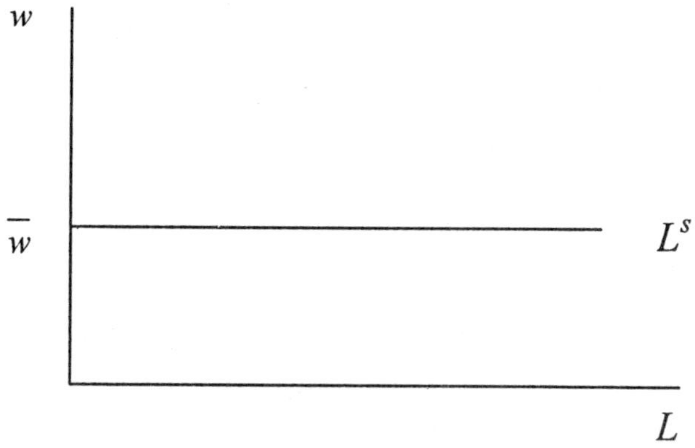

Fig. 1. The Lewis Labour Supply Curve.

The original Lewis supply curve shown above will be modified in two ways. Firstly, two 'turning points' are introduced, the first marking the beginning of a rising supply price phase and the second the full employment level[4]. Next, we allow increases in B-population to add to the supply available for A. With a horizontal supply curve this makes no difference, but once the supply curve starts rising, the turning points are bound to shift to the right with increases in the B-population. To get rid of this complication we will consider the *normalized* supply curve with $\lambda \equiv (L/N)$ on the horizontal axis, where L is employment in A and N the population of B. Full employment means $\lambda = 1$. The normalized supply curve will be independent of N. Therefore, the supply side can be kept stationary and all the dynamics piled upon the demand curve.

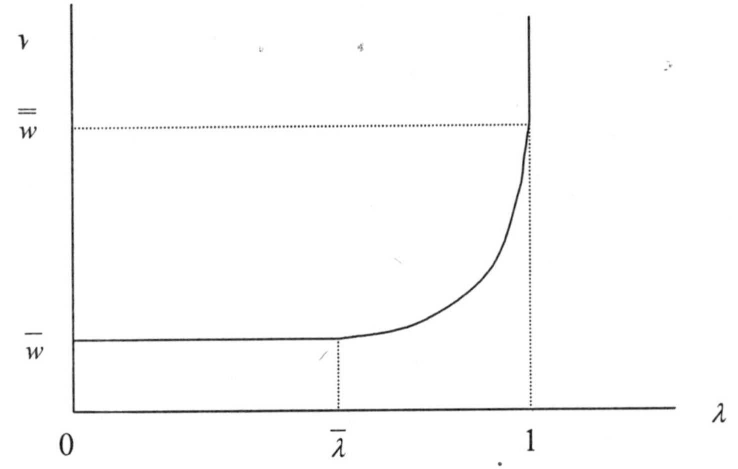

Fig. 2. The Normalized Supply Curve.

2.1 The Demand for Labour from A

Producers in A maximize profit. They set w = MPL by adjusting the r.h.s. taking w to be given. CRS imply that MPL is negatively related to the labour-capital ratio (L/K). The demand for (L/K) depends inversely on w. Denoting $\ell = L/K$, we can write $\ell = \ell(w)$ for the usual labour demand function. The demand curve is downward sloping because of diminishing marginal productivity. The following details are standard.

Profit maximization

Sector A's production function

$F(K, L)$ satisfies constant returns to scale (CRS). Dividing by K we have $F(K, L) = KF(1, \ell)$

Profit is output minus labour cost, and rate of profit is profit per unit of K: $F(K, L) - wL = K[F(1, \ell) - w\ell] = Kr$

Producers maximize r, given K and w. That requires : $F_\ell = w$

CRS implies that F_ℓ depends on ℓ alone. Hence the optimum ℓ depends on w. An increase in w reduces ℓ. This means $L^d = K\ell$ is inversely related to w, and so we have a downward sloping demand curve.

In the short-run, K is historically given, so w fixes L^d. (In general, L^d depends positively on K and negatively on w). For the normalized diagram we need a demand curve relative to the B-population N, i.e. a demand curve in terms of $\lambda = (L/N)$. Given the demand curve in terms of (L/K) we can obtain the demand in terms of λ if we know k, where $k = (K/N)$. This is because $L/N = (L/K)(K/N)$ or $\lambda = \ell k$. Hence the labour demand function in terms of ë is simply the usual labour demand function $\ell(w)$ multiplied by a factor k: $\lambda(w) = k\,\ell(w)$.

Therefore if K rises faster than N then the normalized demand curve $\lambda(w)$ shifts to the right – because k goes up.

The equilibrium level of employment λ will depend on the position of the demand curve. As explained that in turn depends on k. If k is small, the demand-supply intersection takes place on the horizontal stretch of the supply curve and the wage is

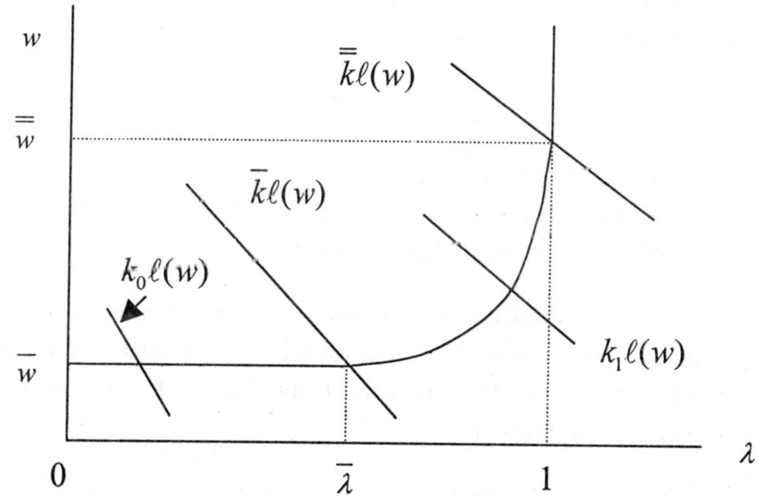

Fig. 3. Possible Equilibria.

exactly the Lewisian minimum $\overline{w}$. If k is large there is full employment with $\lambda = 1$. If k is neither small nor large, the intersection takes place at some intermediate level of employment – with neither surplus labour nor full employment.

To capture the above refer to Fig.3 and introduce 'threshold' capital stocks $\overline{k}$ and $\overline{\overline{k}}$ corresponding to the two turning points.

3. Dynamics

N and K change over time, the former because of exogenous population growth and the latter because of capital accumulation. Only sector A's saving is used for capital accumulation, and that saving comes entirely out of A's profit. For simplicity it is assumed that a constant fraction σ of profit is saved. This fully explains the derivation of the rates of growth of K and k:

$$\dot{K} = \sigma[F(L,K) - wL] = \sigma K[F(\ell,1) - w\ell] = \sigma Kr$$

where r is the rate of profit. Let g_x denote the rate of growth of K.

$$\therefore g_K = \frac{\dot{K}}{K} = \sigma r$$

Note that r depends on w since ℓ depends on w:$r=r(w)$ is a decreasing function of w. Hence g_K is a dcreasing function of w as well : $g_K = \gamma(w)$ with $\gamma'(w) < 0$.

When w is constant over time, so is the rate of growth of K. Thus in this model, the sustainability of growth reduces to asking if w will remain constant or not. There are two ways in which that can happen.

In the first place, labour market equilibrium could continue to occur on the horizontal stretch of the labour supply curve even if k is changing. Start with k_0 in Fig. 3. Increases in K or k would then not affect the wage unless k rises sufficiently to put the economy on the rising segment of the labour supply curve. Thus, if g_K is initially low (relative to population growth n) then k will not rise above k_0. Hence there will be no change in w. Therefore g_K will be constant (i.e. 'growth will be sustainable') if it is initially low. (If at the minimum wage the rate of growth of N were higher than that of K then k will actually fall and the economy will remain trapped in a low-level growth equilibrium).

Constancy of the wage and the growth rate could also result at a wage higher than the minimum. This is the case on a 'steady state' in which the rate of growth of K is equal to that of N so that k is constant. It is to be noted that constancy of the wage rate is a feature of *any* steady state, whether that occurs on the horizontal stretch of the supply curve (is accompanied by surplus labour) or on the rising segment of the curve (with or without full-employment). From this perspective sustainability of growth is by itself no great achievement. Consider this: a steady state is *defined* as a state in which the growth rate is constant – even if it is constant at zero!

Example. To see how growth rates are calculated, consider the example of a Cobb-Douglas production function for sector A:

$$Y = K^{\alpha} L^{\beta} \text{ with } \alpha + \beta = 1$$

$$(Y / K) = \ell^{\beta} \text{ and } r = \frac{\partial Y}{\partial K} = \alpha \frac{Y}{K} = \alpha \ell^{\beta}$$

$$w = \beta \ell^{\beta - 1} = \beta \ell^{-\alpha} \text{ and } w\ell = \beta \ell^{\beta}$$

$$\therefore r = \alpha (\frac{\beta}{w})^{\beta / \alpha} = a(w)^{-\delta} \text{ where } \delta = \beta / \alpha$$

$$\therefore g_K = bw^{-\delta} = c\ell^{\beta}, \text{ where } b = \sigma a \text{ and } c = a\beta$$

3.1 Chalking out growth paths

Start with an initial capital stock k_0 (normalized relative to N). Using Fig. 3, note that associated with any capital stock k is a demand curve $k\ell(w)$ that together with the given labour supply curve determines w. Therefore we can think of a mapping going from k to w thus: $w = w(k)$. Thus, e.g., $w_0 = w(k_0)$.

What does this mapping look like? For small k, as k goes up w remains stuck at its minimum value. After the first turning point, further increases in k raise w. The graph has the same shape as the labour supply curve.

Next invoke the growth function $g_K = \sigma r(w)$ to work out the rate of (proportionate) change over time in K corresponding to any w – such as w_0. We can then figure out the rate of growth of k by netting out the rate of growth of N. Let the latter growth rate be given by a constant n. Then, denoting the rate of growth of k by g, we have

$$g = \sigma r(w) - n = \sigma r(w(k)) - n \equiv g(k)$$

Hence the movement of the economy is determinate. Starting from any k we know how k changes.

The character of the growth path – in particular its limiting value – will depend on certain parameters. Given the production function and the labour supply function, the critical parameters are n and σ. To see this refer to Figs. 4 and 5 and consider the following:

Start with initial k and figure out the corresponding initial w. Note that if $r(w) > n/\sigma$, then $g > 0$ and that means k will rise. If initially w is at its minimum – i.e. k is 'small' – then the rise in k will have no effect on w, but since k will grow at a constant positive exponential rate $[\sigma r - n]$, the first turning point $\bar{k}$ on the supply curve will be reached in finite time and crossed. After that any further increase in k will raise w and bring down

g. Thus whenever $g > 0$, k will rise and push up w. That brings g down. Ultimately the economy will come to rest with $g = 0$. Will this happen at a wage above $\bar{\bar{w}}$ or below?

In Fig. 4 we have shown a particular case where the long run equilibrium is at a wage w^* above $\bar{w}$ and at the same time below the smallest full employment wage. If the minimum wage is relatively "high" (i.e. if $r(\bar{w}) \leq n/\sigma$) then the maximum rate of growth of k will be non-positive. Hence growth will be too weak to take the economy out of the surplus labour phase; surplus labour will be perpetual. Such is the case when n is high or/ and σ is low. On the other hand if the minimum wage is "low" (i.e. if $r(\bar{w}) \leq n/\sigma$) then the steady state will occur beyond the Lewis phase. Starting at the minimum wage, growth will raise k taking it beyond $\bar{k}$. Will the economy hit the full-employment capital stock $\bar{\bar{k}}$ or stop short of it? If at $\bar{\bar{k}}$ the economy's wage is below what is required to bring the growth of K down to n, i.e. below w^*, then k will rise further and the ultimate state must be one of full-employment. But if at $\bar{\bar{k}}$, $g < 0$, then clearly $g = 0$ at a smaller k and the economy will run out steam before full employment is reached.

The Solow model of perpetual full-employment can be generated as a special case in the above scheme when $n/ó$ is low enough so that the steady state wage w^* exceeds the smallest full employment wage $\bar{\bar{w}}$.

To summarize, the steady state is characterized by a constant w – say w^* – such that $\sigma r(w^*) = n$. From Fig. 4 and 5, it is clear that ultimately the capital stock ends up growing at the rate n. The long run equilibrium could be one of three types:

(a) $r(\bar{w}) \leq n/\sigma$: In this case $w^* = \bar{w}$ and there is perpetual surplus labour.

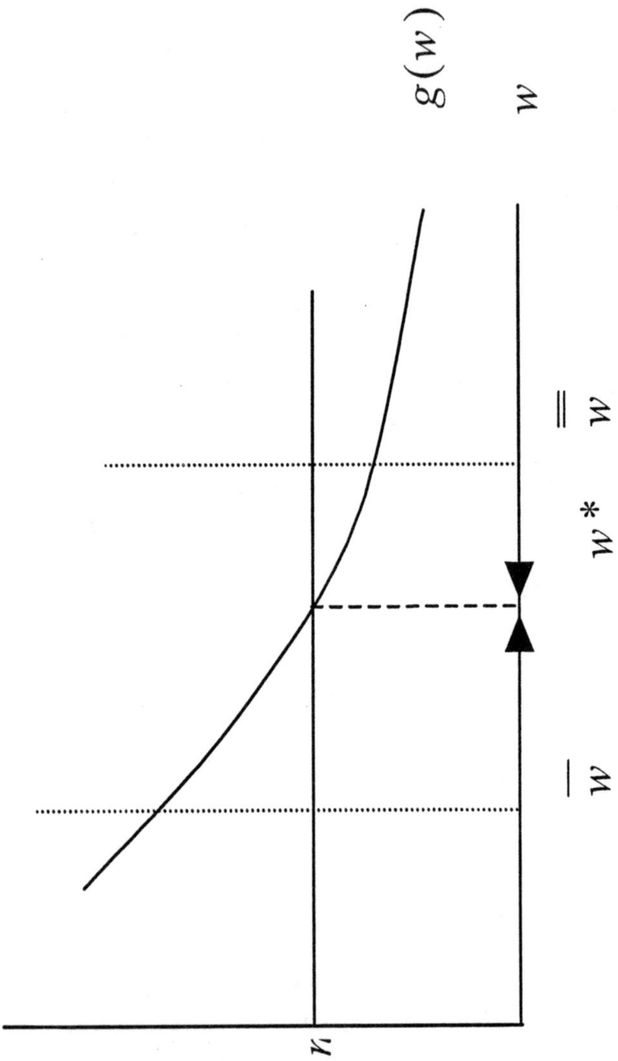

Fig. 4. Long Run Equilibrium.

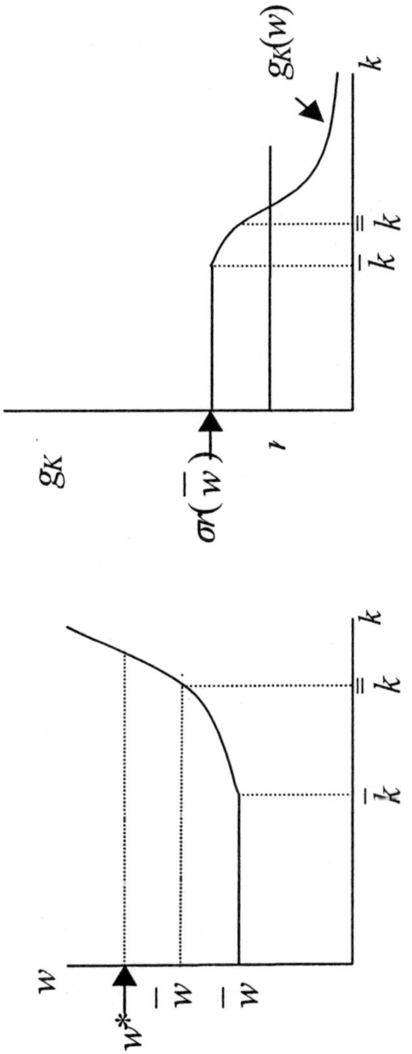

Fig.5. Full Employment in the Lewis model.

(*b*) $r(\bar{w}) > n/\sigma > r(\bar{\bar{w}})$: In this case w^* is larger than the minimum wage but not large enough to yield full employment.

(*c*) $r(\bar{\bar{w}}) \geq n/\sigma$: In this case the long run equilibrium involves full employment and the entire working population has been transferred from B to A.

4. Discussion

The leading question for the discussion is this: what are the lessons from confronting the Lewis model with India's growth experience? The Lewis model builds on 'unlimited supplies' of *unskilled labour* and on growth of the advanced sector being *dependent* on the use of such labour. The key to development here is this dependence of the progressive sector on the backward sector. On the other hand it could happen that, despite the existence of surplus labour, a country's growth is fuelled by activities (e.g., increased exports) that do not require unskilled labour. Instead these activities (exports) may require skilled labour and skilled labour could be scarce – or at least not unlimited. This is a relevant empirical question. If such is the case growth in A doesn't require pulling along B.

But that leads to a different question: Given surplus labour and low wages, why is it *not* profitable for India to export such goods as are intensive in the use of this abundant factor of production? After all, this is exactly what the celebrated Heckscher-Ohlin theory of trade suggests would happen. It may be the case of course that though skilled labour is relatively less cheap in India compared to unskilled labour, Indian skilled labour may still be cheap in comparison to skilled labour in many other countries. This question requires systematic empirical scrutiny.

From this one is led to a general query: has opening up to the external world – globalization – weakened the link between *internal* sectors of the country? If one looks at the Indian scene and reviews the linkage between the traditional and the modern sectors, it seems pretty clear that that linkage has weakened considerably. The changed paradigm of economic development ('services not industry', e.g.) appears to be giving less importance to abundance of unskilled labour. It would seem that opening up provides the modern sector with a new alternative: the opportunity to integrate with the global economy. That changes the preferred pattern of specialization and weakens, if not snaps, its dependence on the traditional sector (for unskilled labour à la Lewis, for instance). There may well be a lot of growth but – as the jargon goes – a lot of 'jobless' growth.

Notes

1. This paper is based on an expository lecture given to undergraduate students at Presidency College.
2. This is different from asking if there exists a method of withdrawing significant amounts of labour from the backward sector without paying higher wages.
3. The classic but controversial definition of 'surplus labour' (tested by Schultz (1964, 1967) and scrutinized by Sen (1966, 1967)) and its proximity to the conc.ept of disguised unemployment a la Joan Robinson (1937) is not directly relevant here.
4. This is standard. See, e.g., Fei and Ranis (1961). .

References

K. Basu (1984) *The Less Developed Economy*, Oxford University Press. New Delhi.

J. C. H. Fei and G. Ranis (1964) *Development of the Labour Surplus Economy: Theory and Policy*, Irwin, Homewood, Ill.

W. A. Lewis (1954) 'Economic Development with Unlimited Supplies of Labour', *Manchester School*, Vol. 32.

D. Ray (1998) Development Economics, Princeton University Press, Princeton, New Jersey.

Joan Robinson (1937) *Essays in the Theory of Employment*, Macmillan, London.

T. W. Schultz (1964), *Transforming Traditional Agriculture*, Yale University Press, New Haven.

__________ (1967), "Significance of India's 1918-19 Losses of Agricultural Labour: A Reply", *Economic Journal*, Vol.77.

Sen, Amartya (1966), 'Peasants and Dualism with or without Surplus Labour', *Journal of Political Economy*, Vol. 74.

__________ (1967), 'Surplus Labour in India: A Critique of Schultz's Statistical Test', Economic Journal, Vol. 77; see also 'A Rejoinder', Economic Journal, Vol. 77.

4

The Way of Industrialization: with Special Reference to India

Paramgama Sikdar, Nikita Modi, Aishani Roy and Debnarayan Sarkar

In the process of industrialization, the nexus between poverty, employment and growth has been the subject matter of intense debate in the recent periods. Basically, two schools of thought have emerged in this context. One school, led by the economists of World Bank-IMF who emphasize economic reforms, and their primary instruments are liberalization, privatization and globalization which could raise the growth rate of GDP. According to this school, unemployment and poverty removal are treated as the corollaries of growth process. (Ahluwalia, 2001; Bhagwati, 1993; Srinivasan, 2000)

It has been argued in the second school that growth per se is not likely to result in a pro-poor growth. In the second school, it has been argued that growth per se is not likely to result in a pro-poor growth to take care of the employment and poverty problem ; so, the content of growth with emphasis on policies which help the poor to become a part of the development process, rather than a residuary beneficiary, is important [Sheila Bhalla (1997), Gilbert (1992), Mahandra Dev (2000), Martin Ravallion and Datt (1999), Abhijeet Sen (1992), Pranab Bardhan (1989), Krishnan (1992) and others]. However, to help the poor become a part of the development process, industrialization should encompass reorganization and reorientation of the entire economic and social systems. To pave the way for this industrialization, illiteracy, unemployment, inequality, and other socio-economic problems of the society should be solved in the best possible way. Thus the aim of this paper is to examine the possible strategies for industrialization necessary for developing countries under the practical framework of the respective countries suited to regional variation of relative factor intensity and relative abundance of factors of production. This study also tries to explore other necessary measures to make such industrialization more equitable and more productive. This study seems to be important in that the strategies for such industrialization might aim at increasing the industrial output of the country leading to sustainable regional development as well as reduction of unemployment, sustained growth in the standard of living, growth for all sectors and all sections along with the augmentation of GDP of the country.

This paper is organized as follows. Section 2 presents the structure of developing economy in Indian context and the need of its industrialization in keeping with its socio-economic conditions. A simple theoretical model appears in section 3 which tries to explore the setting up of different types of industries suited to regional variation of relative factor intensity and relative abundance of factors of production in Indian context. The policy of industrialization in Indian economy and its probable structures are contained in section 4. Section 5 concludes.

Section 2

Notable changes in the structure of GDP and employment pattern have occurred in India over a period of half a century (Table 1). The share of agriculture in GDP has declined to a mere 24 percent in 2004-2005 from 55 percent during 1960-61 periods. That of industry increased from 16 to 25 percent and of services from 29 to 51 percent. This pattern of change has occurred gradually in the span of 50 years. However, such development has accelerated after the economic reforms of 1990-91. In the first forty years, the share of agriculture declined from 59 to 35 percent and in the next 13 years, from 35 to 24 per cent. Share of services increased from 28 to 40 per cent in the first 40 years and from 40 to 51 per cent in the next 13 years. Share of industry has grown slowly but has stagnated since 1990-91.

Table: 1 Shares of different sectors in GDP, employment and ratio of income

SECTOR	*Percentage of employment*		*Share of GDP*		*Ratio of Income*	
	1960-1961	*2004-2005*	*1960-1961*	*2004-2005*	*1960-1961*	*2004-2005*
AGRICULTURAL	74	60	55	24	x	x
INDUSTRIAL	14	18	16	25	x	x
SERVICE	12	22	29	51	x	x
AGRICULTURAL:NON AGRICULTURAL	x	x	x	x	1:3	1:6

Source: Indian Economic Journal, Various Years.

Another significant aspect of India's growth is the shift of labour force with changing sectoral structure of economy. The share of agriculture in the total employment declined from 74 to 60 percent. The shift in labour force has been small as compared to the fall in GDP. In India, industry share in GDP increased from 16 to 25 per cent and employment share from 14 to 18 per cent during 1960-2004. In the case of services, the share of employment has increased far less than increase in share of GDP. In India, while the share of services in GDP increased from 29 per cent in 1960 to 51 per cent in 2004, their share in employment increased from 12 per cent to 22 per cent only.

The growing asymmetry between the sectoral shares of GDP and employment also leads to income inequality. With the fall in share of agriculture in GDP without a corresponding decline in its employment share, the income gap between agriculture and non-agricultural workers is rapidly increasing. With a 55 per cent share in GDP and 74 per cent share in employment, the ratio of per worker agricultural to non-agricultural incomes in 1960 was 1:3; now with 60 per cent workers and 24 per cent GDP in agriculture it is close to 1:6. Ratio between agriculture and services is 1:7 and between agriculture and industry 1:4. With increase in the share of services, this gap will certainly increase unless the growth is accompanied by an increase in the employment share of services.

India followed a path of growth that was mainly service led rather than industry and manufacturing led after the reform of 1991. Availability of skilled labour and improvement in telecommunication triggered the growth of IT industries and exports of IT services. In the developed countries it has been observed that in the initial period's economic development, industries have historically been the main contributor of growth in most of the developed nations of today. However, in India's growth scenario, industries have played only a minor role. In most developed nations of today, service became a predominant sector only after going through a phase of industrialization and industries have attained at least 50 per cent in the economy before the emergence of services as the pre dominant sector. But this unbalanced growth in one sector cannot improve the general standard of living.

Liberalization gave boost to industrialization to some extent; however, to be more cost effective and competitive in export, cost had to be reduced. This led to the retrenchment of labour. Modern and more capital intensive techniques of production were used which led to jobless growth. With the advent of globalization services became predominant and telecom and IT sectors boomed. Such industries required mainly skilled labour and the bulk of semi-skilled and unskilled labour were rendered unemployed or were in the trap of unemployment. The small percent that were employed was due to the trickle down effect. As mentioned earlier, unbalanced growth of skill intensive services cannot lead to improvements in general standard of living.

The structural forms of Indian economy might be also clear from Table 2, representing growth rate of GDP, growth rate of employment and employment elasticity.

This shows that with an increase in the output of service sector, employment opportunity will decrease. Thus, the problem of unemployment will become more acute with further expansion of this sector. The expansion of agricultural sector may not be so optimistic. In this regard the performance of the industrial sector has been better for a labour-intensive country like India; manufacturing field is expected to hold an advantage with regard to absolute level of employment, growth rate of employment and growth rate of GDP.

Is the pattern of industrial growth conducive to the pattern of internal consumption demand? The emerging pattern of growth does seem to be very much compatible with pattern of internal consumption demand. On an average the internal consumption basket of the Indian population, both rural and urban, still consists of mostly agricultural and manufacturing commodities and the share of service is quite small (the share of demand for service sector, for example, is only 26 and 15

Table 2: Growth rate in GDP, employment and employment

	Growth Rate in Employment		*Growth Rate in GDP*		*Employment Elasticity*	
	1983-1993/94	*1993/94-1999/00*	*1983-1993/94*	*1993/94-1999/00*	*1983-1993/94*	*1993/94-1999/00*
AGRICULTURE	2	0	2.9	3.1	0.7	0
MINING	3.7	-1.9	6.2	4.7	.6	-0.4
MANUFACTURING	2.3	2.6	6.1	7.8	0.4	0.3
ELECTRICITY, WATER & GAS	5.3	-3.6	8.4	6.8	0.6	-0.5
CONSTRUCTION	4.2	5.1	4.9	6.3	0.9	0.8
COMMERCE	3.8	5.7	5.6	9.2	0.7	0.6
TRANSPORT	3.3	5.5	6.1	8.7	0.6	0.6
FINANCE	4.5	5.4	10.1	8.4	0.5	0.6
COMMUNITY AND SOCIAL SERVICES	3.9	-2.1	5.7	8.4	0.7	-0.3
TOTAL	2.7	1.1	5.2	6.7	0.5	0.2

percent in urban and rural areas respectively in the year 1999-2000).

Hence the issue is: which sections (sub-sectors) of manufacturing sector need to be given more emphasis based on India's large unemployment, illiteracy, inequality and other socio-economic problems during the current years? Relatively labour intensive industries seem to be more promising in this perspective. The food-processing sector (relatively labour intensive industry) is the largest in terms of number of factories and employment to workers even within the organized sector. Based on data available for 1996-97, presented in Table 3, we provide a brief overview of the selected features of the organized segment of the industry in the various manufacturing sub-sectors. In terms of value of gross output, the Food Processing sector is the second largest among the various sub-sectors in manufacturing in the organized segment but for employment it appears the highest. The relatively low capital requirements and lower labour-skills are indicated by relatively smaller level of fixed assets of the sector (Food Processing) and lower wage rate among the different sub-sectors of manufacturing (these areusually represented by items 20-29 including Food Processing sector).

It is also important to mention that the share of organized sector employment that appears in our earlier discussion plays a very insignificant employment status in the Indian economy. The share of organized sector employment in total employment was of the order of 7.93 percent in 1983, 7.30 in 1994 and 7.08 in 1999-00. However keeping in mind in terms of high proportion of employment, lower fixed capital requirement and lower wage structure, it seems to imply that unorganized rural and urban non-farm industries are best suited for Indian economy. It can not only absorb the abundant resource, unskilled and semi-skilled labour but also increase GDP by raising production. But this should not lead to a situation where small, medium and large manufacturing industries will be neglected. Based on the diversified

Table 3: Description of Factories, Workers, Output, Assets and Wage Rate of different sub-sectors of manufacturing (1996-97)

Item	*Description*	*No. of Factories*	*No. of Workers '000*	*Value of Output Rs. Crore*	*Fixed Assets Rs. Crore*	*Annual wage Rate Rs. '000 Per Worker*
1.	Food Products	22025	995	92404	17075	24
2.	Beverages, tobacco, etc.	8670	542	12090	3486	14
3.	Cotton Textiles	8698	728	34893	14693	31
4.	Wool, Silk, etc.	4103	268	23626	13945	33
5.	Jute Textiles	454	196	3392	943	38
6.	Textiles Products	6098	298	14927	3446	23
7.	Wood, Furniture	3578	62	2156	997	20
8.	Paper & Printing	5048	244	18823	11437	44
9.	Leather & Fur products	11866	109	6423	1369	23
10.	Chemicals, etc.	9286	522	92615	53263	46
11.	Rubber, Petroleum, etc.	7168	261	63248	26875	41

(Contd.)

(Contd. Table 3)

Item	*Description*	*No. of Factories*	*No. of Workers '000*	*Value of Output Rs. Crore*	*Fixed Assets Rs. Crore*	*Annual wage Rate Rs. '000 Per Worker*
12.	Non-metallic mineral products	11279	365	22861	19557	28
13.	Basic Metal Industries	7440	498	70088	53203	57
14.	Metal Products	8176	230	15485	5258	34
15.	Non-electrical machinery, tools and parts	8886	335	38285	9661	53
16.	Electrical machinery	6088	301	38224	11717	48
17.	Transport Equipments	4124	449	51627	16761	48
18.	Other manufacturing	2179	107	8984	2299	36
19.	Repairing Services	2265	208	2928	724	55
	Total	127431	6736	614088	266718	37

regional characteristics, diversification of the setting up of industries in Indian economy seems to be more promising.

Section 3

We make an attempt to develop a theoretical model based on the existing structure of industries of Indian economy. In this theoretical framework we first consider the economy under autarky and then analyze two regions in an economy with differences in relative factor intensity and relative abundance of factors of production, and assume that inter-regional trade between two such economies takes place.

The model we propose is based on the following assumptions:

- **All production functions exhibit constant returns to scale with the property of diminishing marginal returns.**
  This implies that the technology linking the inputs and outputs is such that a given percentage increase in all factors inputs increases output by the same percentage.

- **There is perfect competition in both commodity and factor markets.**
  This implies that the factors of production will be employed and allocated in an optimal manner. There will be no imperfections in the factor or commodity market.

- **There is free trade and goods are freely mobile within regions and sectors with negligible transport costs.**
  This assumption ensures that within an economy, each region will be able to specialize in the production of commodities that require intensive usage of the factor relatively abundant in that region, and the goods are freely mobile inter-regionally.

- **The production functions are such that the two commodities show different factor intensities and there is no factor intensity reversal.**

The feature that distinguishes the two goods or industries is the factor intensity that each requires i.e. the ratio of capital to labour employed in each of the industries. Thus this assumption means that different techniques of production are used in the two industries.

It is imperative to note that elimination of factor intensity reversal will imply that there is one-to-one correspondence between factor intensities and factor prices. In both cases the K/L ratio is an increasing function of the factor price ratio w/r since producers will find it profitable to substitute capital for labour as the relative price of labour rises.

- **The factors are fully employed but not freely mobile between regions and states.**

The immobility of the factor inputs is an important assumption in this model. It is reasonable because different laws of restrictions on factors, different transport costs and different immigration laws persist in different states and so on. But despite different restrictions of the mobility of factor inputs within Indian states, all factors are assumed to be fully employed. It also ensures that the relative endowments of the factor inputs, in this case capital and labour, will remain constant. Abundance is always defined here in relative terms, and not in absolute terms. (According to Paul R. Krugman, *"Abundance is always defined in relative terms, by comparing the ratio of labour to land in the two countries, so that no country is abundant in everything"*). In the context of the following model which explores the relative factor availability in different zones within an economy, the same definition applies to inter-sectorally or inter-regionally.

Moreover the theoretical explanation of Harris and Todaro model (1970) poses some restrictions on the mobility of factor inputs into formal urban sector from informal urban and agricultural sectors (even within different regions of a particular state within India). The following discussions may be of help in examining the validity of this issue.

As is well known, there are two sectors in our economy

1. the formal sector
2. the informal sector comprising of
   - the informal urban sector
   - the agricultural sector

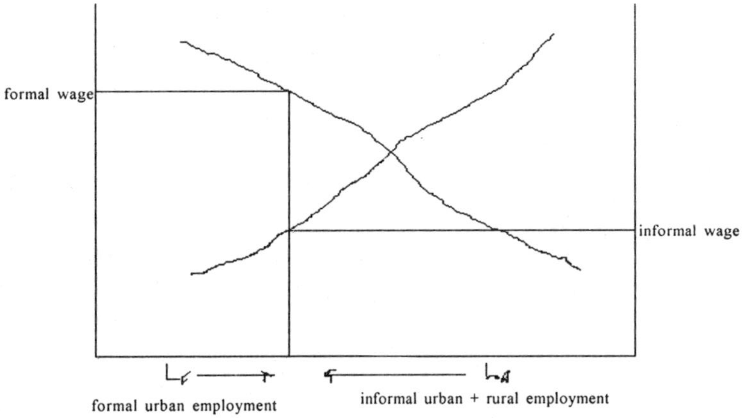

Note: Let L_F, L_I denote employment in the urban formal and informal sectors respectively. Let w_A, w_I and u denote the wage rate in the agricultural, informal urban and formal urban sector. It is to be noted that the wage rate in the formal urban sector is fixed due to urban wage rigidities.

Migration from the rural sector may be thought of as an irreversible decision at least for the proximate future. Because the fate of the potential migrant is not known (i.e. whether he will be employed in the formal urban sector with higher wage or be absorbed into the informal pool with relatively much lower wage), we must consider the expected income from migration and compare it with the actual income received in the agricultural sector. Thus we may conclude that if;

$$\{L_F/(L_F + L_I)\}\, u + \{L_I/(L_F + L_I)\}\, w_I = w_A$$

We are at equilibrium where no person wishes to migrate from one sector to the other. This is the Harris Todaro equilibrium.

It is observed that there is rigidity in the formal urban wage rate which employs and attracts relatively high skilled labour force. In contrast to the high wages with relatively high skilled labour in the formal sector which is unionized, subject to collective bargaining and also treated as a showcase of government policies, the unorganized urban sector and the rural sector employing semi skilled and unskilled labour have low wages that fluctuate according to supply and demand considerations. Hence there is the restriction in the mobility of labour force from the unorganized sector to the formal urban sector. The classical theory of rural and urban migration proposed by Harris and Todaro (1970) clearly points out this phenomenon.

Thus, the assumption of factor immobility within regions or states in an economy might not be unrealistic as is analyzed by Harris Todaro equilibrium condition.

- **Relative price ratio is assumed to be a constant**

Price Index Numbers for Manufactured and Capital Goods in India

Year	*Price Index Number For Manufactured Products (1980-81=100)*	*Price Index Number For Capital Goods (1980-81=100)*	*Relative Price Ratio*
1980-81	100	100	1.0000
1982-83	103.5	102.8	1.0068
1983-84	109.8	106.7	1.0290
1984-85	117.5	112.2	1.0472
1985-86	124.4	121.4	1.0247
1986-87	129.2	127.3	1.0149
1987-88	138.5	132.3	1.0468
1988-89	151.6	150.8	1.0053

(Contd.)

(Contd. Table)

Year	*Price Index Number For Manufactured Products (1980-81=100)*	*Price Index Number For Capital Goods (1980-81=100)*	*Relative Price Ratio*
1989-90	168.6	166.2	1.0144
1990-91	182.8	180.2	1.0144
1991-92	203.4	208.3	0.9764
1992-93	225.6	230.6	0.9783
1993-94	243.2	237.9	1.0222
1994-95	268.6	262.8	1.0220
1995-96	293.1	282.8	1.0364
1996-97	305	295	1.0338
1997-98	317.5	299.4	1.0605
1998-99	331.9	304.7	1.0892
1999-00	333.6	276.2	1.2078

Source: Indian Economic Journal.

From the fourth column of the above table we observe that the relative price ratio has remained fairly constant over the years. Thus, the assumption holds. This table also lends credence to the fact that as the relative price index between manufactured product and capital goods product is more or constant, the relative price index between labour intensive manufactured product and capital goods product might be more or less constant for these periods (1980-81 to 1999-00).

We are considering a region having relative abundance in labour. It produces two commodities X, capital intensive and Y labour intensive good respectively. Here labour and capital are the only two inputs used in the production process.

It is known to all that there exists a one to one relation between relative prices of the goods and their factor price ratio. Again as we fix the relative price ratio the ratio of capital to labour used also gets fixed.

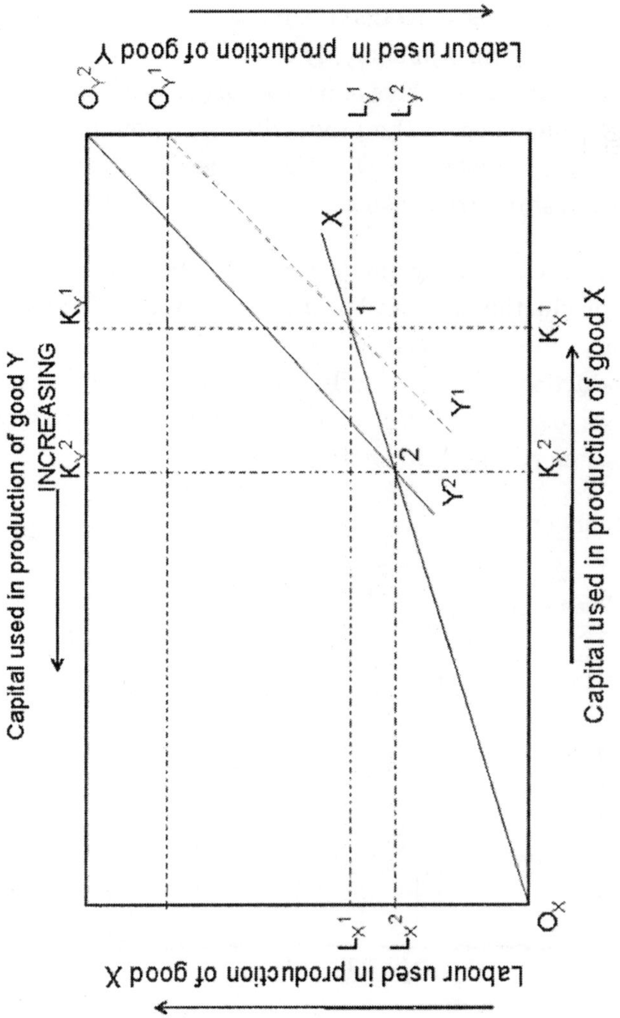
Labour used in production of good Y
Labour used in production of good X
Capital used in production of good Y
INCREASING
Capital used in production of good X
X
Y1
Y2
1
2

Now let us consider the allocation of resources at given prices. The region considered has relative abundance in labour and the technology adopted is labour intensive.

In the diagram we show that the initial resource allocation point is 1. At given prices and supply of capital if the supply of labour increases then we arrive at a very surprising result. The quantity of labour used in the production of Y now has to be measured from OY^2 instead of OY^1. Consequently the resource allocation point shifts from 1 to 2.

It is observed that the amount of both labour and capital used in the production of X and therefore the total production of X, the capital intensive good, actually falls. The surplus inputs from the production of X are actually soaked up in the production of Y. Needless to say that the production of the labour intensive good, Y, rises more than proportionately.

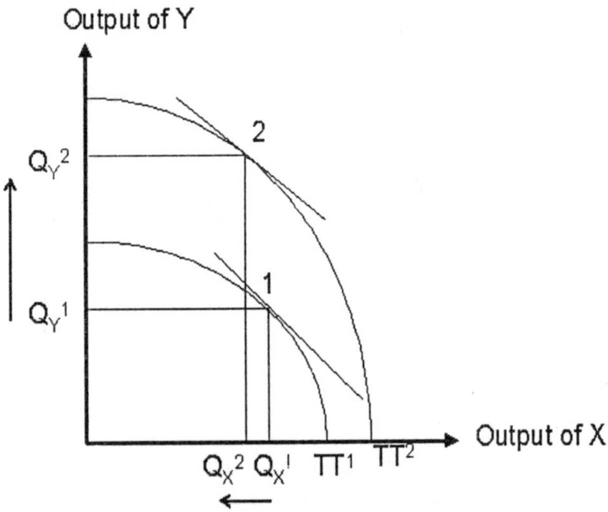

The initial ppf is given by TT^1. Initially output is produced at point 1, where the slope of ppf equals $-P_X/P_Y$, with the rise in supply of labour the ppf shifts to TT^2. Production of both X and

Y could have been boosted. However we observe a biased expansion of production possibilities. Relative prices remaining constant production moves from point 1 to 2 leading to a fall in output of X and huge rise in that of Y.

The following proof shows that a labour intensive industry is more suitable in a region which has relative abundance in labour.

Let us consider two commodities X and Y. Y is labour intensive where is X is capital intensive.

We define the following terms:

L: total supply of labour

K: total supply of capital

α_{LY}: share of labour used for production of Y

α_{LX}: share of labour used for production of X

α_{KY}: share of capital used for production of Y

α_{KX}: share of capital used for production of X

$\alpha_{LY} > \alpha_{KY}$ and $\alpha_{LX} < \alpha_{KX}$

$\alpha_{LY} + \alpha_{LX} = 1$ and $\alpha_{KY} + \alpha_{KX} = 1$

Q_x and Q_y are the amounts of X and Y produced.

Factor prices remaining unchanged the changes in output can be expressed in terms of changes in the factor inputs by the two following equations:

$$\alpha_{LX}\hat{Q}_X + \alpha_{LY}\hat{Q}_Y = \hat{L}$$

$$\alpha_{KX}\hat{Q}_X + \alpha_{KY}\hat{Q}_Y = \hat{K}$$

On solving and simplification we get

$$\hat{Q}_Y = \hat{L} + \frac{\alpha_{LX}}{\Delta}(\hat{L} - \hat{K})$$

$$\hat{Q}_X = \hat{K} - \frac{\alpha_{KY}}{\Delta}(\hat{L} - \hat{K})$$

Thus if the supply of labour in production rises we get:

$$\hat{Q}_Y > \hat{L} > \hat{K} > \hat{Q}_X$$

Thus the change in output is greater than the change in employment of the abundant factor. If output changes significantly then change in employment will be considerable too.

Hence, we have shown that an economy will be relatively effective at producing goods that are intensive in the factors with which the country is relatively well endowed.

The comparison can be extended between different states: one state having relatively labour abundance than the other state having relatively capital abundance. So that the former might produce relatively labour intensive goods (and the latter will produce relatively capital intensive goods) and exchange it for more capital intensive goods from the latter.

Now suppose the production possibility frontier for an economy producing X and Y is

$$x_p^2 + y_p^2 = 100 \qquad ...(i)$$

Where, x_p and y_p are the amounts of X and Y are the amounts of X and Y produced.

Then the slope of the tangent at any point on product transformation curve is the rate at which good Y must be sacrificed in order to obtain additional unit of X without varying the 100 units of inputs used. The negative of the slope is defined as the rate of product transformation

$$RPT = -dy_p/dx_p \qquad \text{...(ii)}$$

Suppose the particular economy values its output at fixed prices. The linear equation of its iso-revenue curve is given by:

$$x_pP_x + y_pP_y = V \qquad \text{...(iii)}$$

It is the basic proposition of microeconomics that, any market that is not distorted by monopoly or other market failures has an objective of maximization of value of output at given market prices.

We form the Lagrangian equation:

$W = x_pP_x + y_pP_y + \lambda(100 - x_p^2 - y_p^2)$: λ being the Lagrange multiplier

FOC's are as follows:

$$\delta w/\delta x_p = P_x - 2\lambda x_p = 0$$

$$\delta w/\delta y_p = P_y - 2\lambda y_p = 0$$

And,

$$\delta w/\delta\lambda = 100 - x_p^2 - y_p^2 = 0$$

We assume that SOC holds.

Therefore, $P_x/P_y = x_p/y_p$ ... (iv)

The point at which the economy will produce is the point where the value of output is maximum.

We now consider the demand condition for X and Y of the economy.

Let the utility function be of the form

$$U = x_c y_c \quad ..(v)$$

Where x_c and y_c are the amounts of X and Y consumed.

As the value of an economy's quantity consumed equals the value of output produced, we get,

$$X_p P_x + Y_p P_y = P_x x_c + P_y Y_c = 100 \quad ... (vi)$$

This equation shows that the production and consumption lines must lie on the same isovalue line. The economy tries to maximize its consumption subject to the utility function.

$$V = P_x x_c + P_y Y_c + \lambda(U_o - x_c y_c)$$

The FOC's are:

$$\delta v/\delta x_c = P_x - \lambda y_c = 0$$

$$\delta v/\delta y_c = P_y - \lambda x_c = 0$$

$$\delta v/\lambda\delta = U_o - x_c y_c = 0$$

We assume that SOC holds.

Therefore, $P_x/P_y = y_c/x_c$ ..(vii)

It occurs that point on the line which touches the PPF (without exchange condition).

$$-dy_p/dx_p = x_p/y_p = P_x/P_y = y_c/x_c = \mu \text{ (say)} \quad ...(viii)$$

Therefore,

$$x_p/y_p = \mu$$

or, $x_p = \mu y_p$

Putting the value of x_p in the equation of PPF or product transformation curve, we get,

$$(\mu y_p)^2 + (y_p)^2 = 100$$

or, $$(\mu^2 + 1)y_p^{\,2} = 100$$

or, $$y_p^* = 10/(1+\mu^2)^{1/2}$$

or, $$x_p^* = 10\,\mu/(1+\mu^2)^{1/2}$$

We have shown how to find out an economy's production and consumption given relative prices in autarky.

Trade can be defined as the difference between production and consumption.

In an offer curve diagram we show directly the trade flows that correspond to any given relative price. The more labour abundant country makes the offer $(y_p - y_c)$ units of Y for $(x_c - x_p)$ units of X.

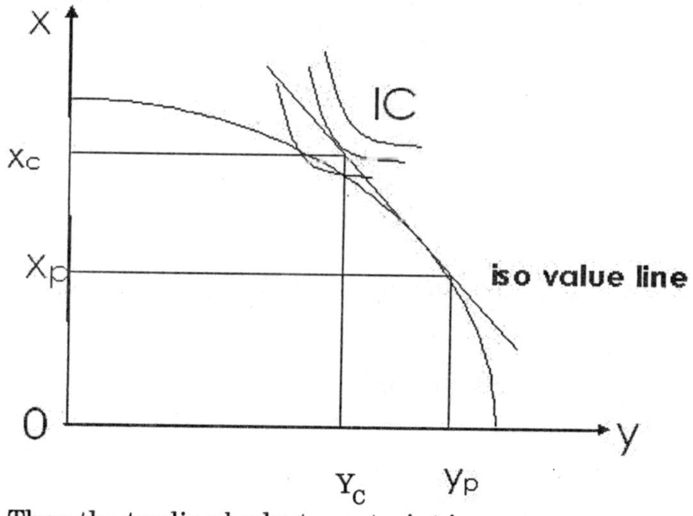

Then the trading budget constraint is

$$y_p - y_c = (x_c - x_p) \times \frac{P_x}{P_y}$$

$$\text{or, } \mu(x_c - x_p) - y_p - y_c \qquad (\because \frac{P_x}{P_y} = \mu)$$

$$\text{or, } \mu x_c + y_c = \mu x_p + y_p$$

$$\text{or, } \mu x_c + y_c = \frac{10\mu^2}{\sqrt{1+\mu^2}} + \frac{10}{\sqrt{1+\mu^2}}$$

$$= \frac{10(1+\mu^2)}{\sqrt{1+\mu^2}}$$

$$\therefore \mu x_c + y_c = 10\sqrt{1+\mu^2}$$

This budget constraint means that the value of export equals the value of import. The continuity marginal rate of substitution (MRS) is given by the equation...(viii)

$$\frac{y_c}{x_c} = \frac{p_x}{P_y} = \mu$$

$$\therefore y_c = \mu x_c$$

Putting the value of y_c in the budget constraint of trade we get

$$\mu x_c + \mu x_c = 10\sqrt{1+\mu^2}$$

$$\text{or, } x_c = \frac{5\sqrt{1+\mu^2}}{\mu} \quad \therefore y_c = \sqrt{1+\mu^2}$$

We have $y_p = \frac{10}{\sqrt{1+\mu^2}}$, $x_p = \frac{10\mu}{\sqrt{1+\mu^2}}$

$y_c = 5\sqrt{1+\mu^2}$ and $x_c = \frac{5\sqrt{1+\mu^2}}{\mu}$

∴ The traded quantities of the goods are

$$y_p - y_c = \frac{10}{\sqrt{1+\mu^2}} - 5\sqrt{1+\mu^2}$$

$$= \frac{10 - 5 - 5\mu^2}{\sqrt{1+\mu^2}} = \frac{5(1-\mu^2)}{\sqrt{1+\mu^2}}$$

$$x_c - x_p = \frac{5\sqrt{1+\mu^2}}{\mu} - \frac{10\mu}{\sqrt{1+\mu^2}}$$

$$= \frac{5(1+\mu^2) - 10\mu^2}{\mu\sqrt{1+\mu^2}}$$

$$= \frac{5(1-\mu^2)}{\mu\sqrt{1+\mu^2}}$$

When $\mu < 1$, the exports (or imports) of goods y (or x) are positive. For $\mu > 1$ the reverse occurs. For different values of μ we plot the export of one goods against the import of the other goods we get the following offer curves:

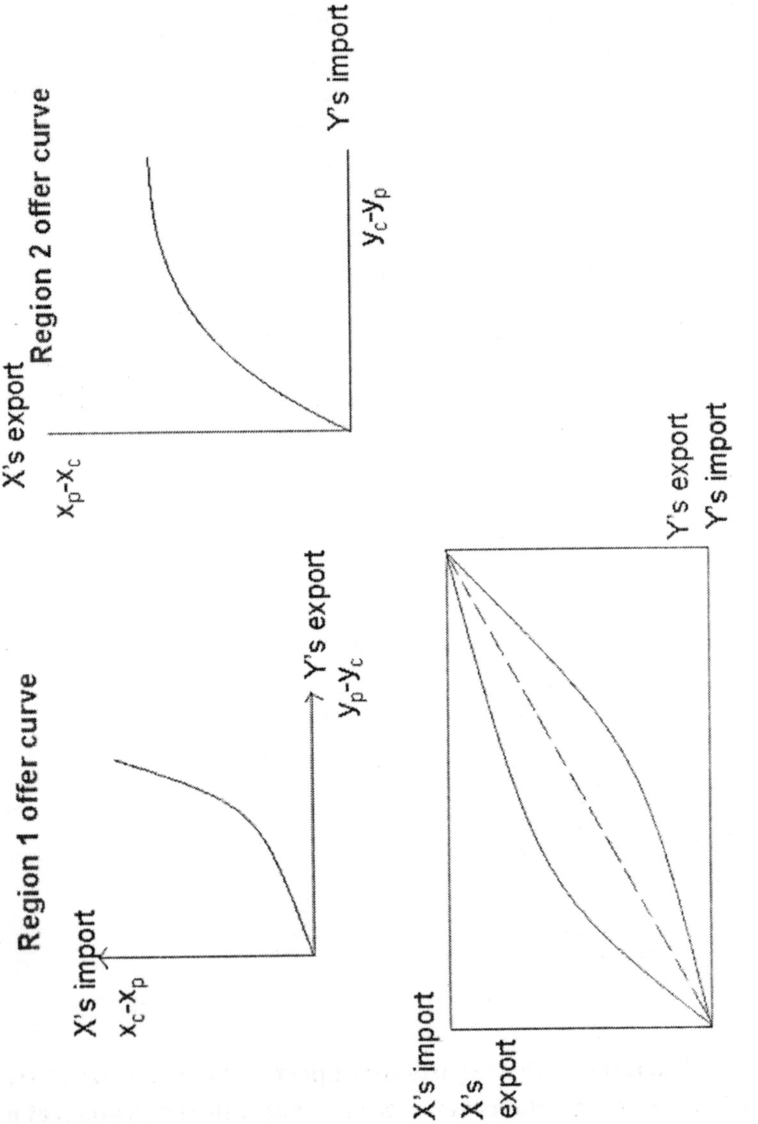
Region 2 offer curve
X's export
x_p-x_c
Y's import
y_c-y_p
Region 1 offer curve
X's import
x_c-x_p
Y's export
y_p-y_c
Y's export
Y's import
X's import
X's
export

Equilibrium is at the point where the home and the foreign offer curves intersect. The point of intersection of the two offer curves gives the point at which exchange actually takes place. It is a situation in which both countries will gain from the trade. In other words, there may be gains to all parties from the exchange.

Although it is said that factor proportion theory is more applicable for different countries, the reference of this theory seems to be more pronounced with the existing situation of Indian states. Both skilled and unskilled labour persists in the economy. Moreover, the existence of more than one hundred and ten crores of people, clearly indicates that production, consumption and exchange of both types of goods (or different types of goods) are also possible across regions or states within our country. If this policy is taken with consideration, growth of both relatively labour and capital intensive industries might accelerate without compromising the growth of employment of both labour and capital. In other words both types of industries (or many other industries) might accelerate growth of GDP with simultaneous growth of employment for both labour and capital.

More importantly, although the comparative advantage trade theory of this paper which offers gains from specialization given regional current situation within a country, but such a specialization for different types of industries conducive to different regions of a country (inter-regional trade within a country) may leave open the possibility for gains from increasing returns, usually stemming from falling average costs, for some manufactured commodities from international trade between countries in future. It might support some modalities of new trade theory (NTT) induced by larger markets and greater specialization(Dixit and Stiglitz, 1977; Krugman,1979; Bernard et al, 2007). But to pave the way for this dynamic expansion induced by larger markets with greater specialization, government have to comply with some industries' demand for temporarily protection, subsidies and infrastructural investment.

Section 4

The labor force and the type of industries required

India has a pool of unskilled labour force either unemployed or underemployed. For sustainable industrialization to happen in India, this pool of unskilled labour has to be put in productive employment. We also discuss that as a country enters the phase of industrialization, the share of agriculture has to go down. So in India, the development of non farm industries is the key to effective industrialization. Rural non farm industry typically requires semi skilled or unskilled laborers. Hence, they can absorb the abundant laborers from unproductive agricultural sector and help to alleviate rural poverty, make income distribution more equitable and also contribute to economic growth. This will also lead to diversification of income sources. Also it will restrict the migration of rural workers to the cities. The industries that are established in an around cities can then, at feasible pace, absorb the already existing labour force. This will reduce excess supply of labour thereby increasing the wage rate. Hence, the labour intensive non farm industries are the key to sustainable industrialization. What is rural non farm activities composed of ? There are diverse definitions of rural non farm activities. Broadly, it is composed of manufacturing, trade, construction, transportation, communication and services. Also, income earned by rural families making handicrafts and other petty products also fall in this category.

The demand factor

There are two sources of demand for non farm products; the demand of farm households for consumer goods and the demand of urban households for process agricultural goods. As mentioned earlier, there is heavy demand of agricultural and manufactured goods by both urban and rural population. This demand can be met by the expansion of the non farm sector.

The expansion of the rural non farm sector will also create demand by increasing the purchasing power of the rural population. This will be achieved by the following mechanism. With the expansion of the rural non farm sector, rural income will rise which in turn will increase the purchasing power of the people influencing thereby to step up the demand for goods from the non farm sector. Farm households in India are mainly small and medium sized. These households have high demand for non farm consumption goods. As agricultural output increases, demand for agricultural inputs like fertilizers and other non farm implements will increase. Thus Food Processing and Agricultural Inputs manufacturing are the key non farm industries that will not only meet rural demand but also create additional demand and help the basis for future expansion and these might help improve living standards of the people in a sustainable manner.

The absence of non farm sector increases disguised unemployment and causes migration. For example, in the semi arid region of western India, the absence of a dynamic non farm sector pushes people into unproductive farm activities where they have practically negative or zero marginal productivity. In such cases people are fast migrating to urban areas in search of work.

It is important to note that a blind promotion of such rural nonfarm industries without adequate linkages will not be feasible or economically viable. Such industries should be set up which work in conjunction with the urban industries. These industries may produce inputs and components required in the capital intensive urban industries or even assemble their finished products.

Infrastructure

Setting up industries without meeting the basic infrastructural requirements will not only be a waste of resources but will also be unsustainable in the long run. The most primary requirement is of course a good network of roads for quick delivery of inputs and finished products to and from the market. This will reduce labour costs considerably. It will increase the marketability of the product and also in development of inter-regional trade. Out of nearly 6 lakh villages, only 60% are known to be connected by all-weather roads at the beginning of the Ninth Plan. In UP, for instance, inadequate infrastructure in general, and in particular, the decreasing availability and reliability of power supply and water for irrigation have lowered productivity in agriculture and industry, thereby contributing to lower rates of poverty reduction. Electricity, road density and banking facilities explain most of the variation in industrial development across districts.

Another primary infrastructural requirement is the continuous supply of power. The continuous hindrance to power supply means that the factories have to often rely on diesel and other fuels which is a huge bottleneck that reduces productivity and efficiency.

The power sector faces an imminent crisis in almost all states. No State Electricity Board (SEB) is recovering the full cost of power suppy with the result that they make continuous losses on their total operations. The annual losses of SEBs at the end of the Ninth Plan were Rs 24,000 crores and this has led to large outstanding dues to Central PSUs NTPC, NHPC, CIL, Railways, etc. amounting to Rs. 35,000 crores. SEB overcharge industry and commercial users, but these do not always pay the high charges because here also lies the existence of theft of electricity, typically with the connivance of the staff in the distribution segment. Government has also failed to attract private investors in power generation, as the independent power producer cannot be expected to sell power to a public sector distributor, who is not in a position to pay for the power purchased. The result has been that the inflow of private investment has been much below the targeted level.

It is important to consider is that the infrastructure required differs from product to product. It is extremely difficult to make available such product specific infrastructure. It requires not only detailed industry assessment but the process should also be continuous to incorporate technological progress. The government should promote private parties or traders or producers association to provide such specific infrastructure like cool vans, quality control labs and processing units.

Education and Training

Education and training is an essential tool to facilitate industrialization in the long run and sustain immediate ventures. While primary and secondary education will create a pool of workforce for the future, vocational and job training will create a technically sound workforce for the present. Literacy will enhance the quality of production and will promote technological know how. It will lead to better understanding of production techniques which will increase the efficiency per worker.

Such provisions have been undertaken by the government which has established District Industry Centres (DIC), Industrial Training Institutes (ITIs), rural poly-technics but they are highly inefficient in their functioning. They should be restructured so that they may cater to the local needs. They should also be adequately staffed and provided with adequate resources so that they can maintain a continuous process of assessment and can identify newer trades for training taking note of the resource endowment of the region.

With globalization and economic liberalization there have arisen a host of new opportunities which should be tapped by these organizations and translated into opportunities.

Credit

The rural non farm sector is highly capital deficient. Financial institutions fail to identify their target lending sectors. Also the procedures are very rigid and inefficiency in functioning leads to long lags in the allocation of funds. Easy availability of credit will give an impetus to the growth of non farm industries and will also give a boost to local entrepreneurs. This problem can be solved by establishing and encouraging community collaterals. The Self Help Groups (SHG's) can viably serve the needs of small scale finances. They can also help in dissemination of knowledge regarding better production techniques. The performance of the non-banking financial institutions in allocating credit to the SHG's has been unsatisfactory. Development of regional rural banks, increasing the number of branches will help organized disbursement of credit.

The role of the government

It is not possible for the central government to be well versed with the needs of different settlements across the countries. For effective and sustainable solution to problems, decentralization of power is an absolute must. The local governments should be given the power and the finances to promote the rural non farm sector. Decentralization of decision making is required. Local governments can speedily supply managerial and seed capital. Once established, these ventures can turn into well established small private enterprises.

Government should lay its focus on basic infrastructure like power, road and communication and such facilities should remain in public domain. The scope of the Rural Infrastructure Development Fund can be expanded by instituting policies allowing it to make investments in fields other than irrigation.

A Bharat Nirman program should be launched that specifically targets the development of rural non farm sector.

Traditionally, the state is perceived as the provider of infrastructure and state-borne institutions as the creator of rural technology. This perception is however changing with the emergence of new institutional alternatives. The sustenance of such institutions also requires government support, which may be in the form of a suitable legislative environment, fewer functional bottlenecks and faster redress of grievances. Government policies that may increase the capabilities of workers by providing better education and health facilities should be encouraged. Worthwhile to mention that the government has proposed several schemes to promote the nonfarm sector:-

- Creating entrepreneurship through subsidized loans (IRDP, SGSY, PMRY)
- Provide skills (TRYSEM, ITI)
- Strengthen gender component (DWCRA, RMK)
- Provide wage employment (JRY, EAS, Food for Work, SJRY)
- Industry specific schemes (Khadi and handloom products)

Government sponsored schemes have achieved only marginal success. The principal reason behind this is the multiplicity of schemes and the absence of any effective follow up mechanism. The schemes are not coordinated or routinely administered. The proper implementation requires continuous assessment, surveillance and administration.

The Role of NGO's

There are bottlenecks in every step. The participation of Non Governmental Organizations or NGO's will lead to better implementation of these programmes.

The rural sector in India has a large number of artisans. In this changing world, the demand for some products of the artisans' work has declined, while that of some other skill-intensive, artisan-like work has increased; such shifts in demands need to be assessed. In a liberalizing world, when distance is shrinking there may be a latent demand for an artisan's work in a distant market, the tapping of which requires the help of market professionals. In the context of emerging opportunities rural artisans abilities may be increased on a selective basis; while care is taken to ensure that this training is integrated with the production and marketing of such products. Though some public institutions such as the KVIC have been mandated for similar purposes, they have failed miserably in performing their role. There is a need for alternate institutions and producers' associations to undertake the job of training, producing and marketing the rural artisan's products. NGOs may encourage the formation of producers' SHGs to share the benefits of lucrative prices in distant markets.

Section 5

This paper might suggest that although factor proportion theory is more applicable for cross-country situation, the existing situation of our economy, where both skilled and large unskilled labour simultaneously persist in the economy with the existence of more than one hundred crores of people, production, consumption and exchange of various types of industrial goods are possible across regions or states within our country. This paper also prescribes other necessary measures (infrastructure, education and training, credit, roles of government and NGO's) to make such industrialization more equitable and more productive. The strategies for such industrialization might help at increasing the industrial output of the country leading to sustainable regional development as well as reduction of unemployment, sustained growth in the slandered of living, growth for all sectors and all sections along with the augmentation of GDP of the country.

This paper might also suggest that if such a specialization for different types of industries conducive to different regions takes place, it may leave open the possibility for gains from increasing returns, usually stemming from falling average costs, from international trade between countries for some manufactured commodities leading to support some modalities of new trade theory (NTT) induced by larger markets and greater specialization in future. But to pave the way for this dynamic expansion induced by larger markets with greater specialization, the government has to comply with some industries' demand for temporary protection, subsidies and infrastructural investment.

References

Ahluwalia, M.S. (2001): Economic Reference of States in Private Reform Period under Education in *National Human Development Report, 2002*, New Delhi, Oxford University Press.

Bardhan, P (1989): "*Poverty and Employment Characteristics of Urban Households in West Bengal:* An Analysis of the Results of National Sample Survey, 1977-78", G. Rodgers (ed.), Urban Poverty and the Labor Market, *International Labor Office*, Geneva.

Bernard, A B, J B Jensen, S J Redding and P K Schott (2007) : " Firms in International Trade" in *Journal of Economic Perspectives*, 21: 105-130.

Bhagwati, J.N. (1993): "*India in Transition: Freeing the Economy*", Clarendon Press.

Bhalla, S (1997): "Trends in Poverty, Wages and Employment in India, *Indian Journal of Labour Economics*", Volume 40, No. 2.

Bhaumik S.K. (2007): Growth and Composition of Rural Non –Farm Employment in India,*The Indian Economic Journal,* Vol. 55, No. 3, Oct-Dec.

Dev, M (2000): "Economic Liberalization and Employment in South Asia", *Economic and Political Weekly*, January 15.

Dixit, Avinash, K and Joseph E Stiglitz (1977): "Monopolistic Competition and Optimum Product Diversity", *The American Economic Review*, 67(3): 297-308.

Etienne, G (1997): "Agricultural Policies and Development in South Asia", *South Asian Survey,* Vol. 4, No. 1, 95-108.

Etienne, G (1992): "*The Steel Industry in China and India* by Gilbert Eitenne (ed)", Sage Publication, London.

Islam, N (1997): "The Non Farm Sector and Rural Development: Review of Issues and Evidences"; *International Food Policy Research Institute*, Food, Agriculture and the Environment Discussion Paper No. 22.

Jha, B (2006): "Rural Non-Farm Employment in India: Macro-trends, Micro-evidences and Policy Options", *IEG Working Paper Series* No. E/272/2006.

Kalirajan, K. and S. Bhide; (2007): "Sources of Growth in the Indian Food Processing Sector: A Frontier Production Function Analysis", *The Indian Economic Journal*, Volume 55, Number 2, July-September.

Krishnan, J.N. (1992): "Population, Poverty and Employment in India", *Economic and Political Weekly*, Nov. 14.

Krugman, P R (1979): "Increasing Returns, Monopolistic Competition and International Trade", *Journal of International Economics*, 9, 469-79.

Mukherjee, A, X. Zhang (2005): "*Rural Non farm Development in China and India: The Role of Policies and Institutions*", International Food Policy Research Institute; Development Strategy and Governance Division, Discussion Paper No. 24.

Nagaraj, R (2005): "Industrial Growth in China and India": *Economic and Political Weekly,* May 21.

Nagaraj, R (2007): "*Labour Market in India: Current Concerns and Policy Responses*"; Seminar on Labour Markets in Brazil, China and India; Organization for Economic Cooperation and Development.

Papola, T.S. (2005): "*Emerging Structure of Indian Economy: Implications of Growing Intersectoral Imbalances*", Presidential Address of 88th Annual Conference of Indian Economic Association, 27–29 December, 2005, Vishakhapatanam.

Radhakrishna, R (2002): "Agricultural Growth, Employment and Poverty", *Economic and Political Weekly,* January 19.

Ravellion, M and G Datt (1999): "When is Growth Pro-Poor? Evidence from Divine Experience of India's States", *World Bank Policy Research Working Paper*, M2263.

Srinivasan, T.N. (2000): *Eight Lectures on India's Economic Reform*, New Delhi, Oxford University Press.

SECTION - III

5

Priority Policy Objectives of West Bengal Left Front Government in the Process of Agriculture- Industry Interactions

Debnarayan Sarkar and Debraj Das

There have been a few attempts to formulate a theory of macroeconomic policy planning for framing suitable government policy targets in different countries. One of the first explicit attempts in this perspective was undertaken by Timbergen (1952,1956). The 'standard optimizing framework' is the theoretical foundation of Timbergen's work. The explicit assumption of this framework is that policy makers adopt an objective function which is characterized by continuous substitution between objectives of macro policy. Subsequently others works, that appear in this line, are of Theil (1956,1968), Fisher (1968, 1970), Pissarides (1972), Peston (1974), Kydland and Prescott (1977), Currie and Levine (1985) and others.

However during the last two decades there have been a number of criticisms against the standard approach. 'Satisficing' approach to economic policy, one of the few attempts for framing government's economic policy, takes into account most of the criticism and tries to remove those difficulties. This approach draws from the works of Mosley (1976), Mosley and Cracknell (1984) Frey (1978), Frey and Schneider (1978) and others. Most importantly, 'satisficing' approach takes into account the problems concerning symmetries and the role of socio-economic pressure groups. In addition, the framework contains the sequential attention to goals, which implies that there is no continuous substitution among policy makers objectives.Instead of continuous substitution of policy making objectives, 'satisficing' approach contains the idea of sequential attention to goals and extends this into a priority based choice model of government behaviour. There are indications of the empirical relevance of such models (Frey and Ramser,1978, Alesina,1987, Alesina and Saches, 1988). It implies that there are more important goals or targets (or given levels of important variables) that need to be satisfied first before secondary ones (or other less important variables) are considered. In keeping with this, this paper also tries to formulate a simple theoretical framework of priority-policy objectives for Government of West Bengal in the process of interactions between agriculture and industry of the state of West Bengal in Indian context. This study seems to be important in that this government have been ruling the State for a longer period (about 32 years) since 1977 at a stretch and from the very beginning of their activities this government have been executing one set of priority-policy objective: (increase employment generation to the maximum extent possible and through that, increase income for reducing poverty, i.e. employment generation, increase in income and poverty reduction)[1]. Here the most important policy object is the increase in employment, which might lead to increase in income and thereby reduce the level of poverty, and this needs to be satisfied first (or the qualitative improvement of people or human development issues need to be satisfied first), before the growth issues are considered. Worthwhile to mention that the 'satisficing' model support the view that the party in power will set target levels of priority policy objectives in order to satisfy its electoral support and increases the chances of re-election.

This paper proceeds as follows. Section 1 presents a theoretical model related to priority policy objectives of Left Front Government of West Bengal. Section 2 outlines the performance of West Bengal in these perspectives. Section 3 concludes.

1. Theoretical Framework

As mentioned earlier given levels of important variables (for example, employment related issues) must be satisfied first before other less important variables (for example, growth issues) are considered. Let a and a' be two alternatives which might be bundles of goods with respect to macroeconomic policy objectives.

$$a = (a_1, a_2, a_3, \ldots, a_n)$$

$$a' = (a'_1, a'_2, a'_3, \ldots, a'_n)$$

a p a' iff (p means preferred to)

1. $a_1^* > a_1 > a_1'$ or

2. $a_1 = a_1' < a_1^*$; $a_2 > a_2'$, or

3. $a_1' < a_1^* < a_1$, or

4. $a_1^* < a_1, a_1'$; $a_2^* > a_2 > a_2'$.

....

$a_{n-1}^* < a_{n-1}, a_{n-1}'$; $a_n > a_n'$.

The starred variables represent acceptable or satisfactory level of goods, which of course in line with other work on satisficing, need not be fixed. Component a_1 is considered as more important than a_2 up to a point where $a_1 > a^*$. The same holds well for a_2 up to a_n. This preference system is likely to produce kinked indifference curves. The sequential character of the social utility function can be useful when there are multiple objectives, especially in relation with the macroeconomic policy where constraints are common. We assume that there are two macroeconomic goals employment (E) and growth (G) and that employment is the primary policy objective until E*, then we can express the above by taking a two point function:

$$U(E,E^*,G)= \{U_1(E,G), U_2(E,E^*, G)\}$$

Where $U(E, E^*, G)=U_1$ for $E<E^*$ and

$$U(E,E^*,G)= U_2 \text{ for } E \geq E^*$$

The appropriate level of E* represents compromise among government units (or lobbying groups). Following Black on voting and preferences, the social E*, for instance, could be the median of individual candidates for E*. In case there is a secondary target (e.g. G*), the process can be repeated.

Following Mankiw (1988), we can construct the utility function as,

$$E + cG^2 \quad \text{for } E<E^*$$

$$U =$$

$$E^* + cG^2 + \alpha(E-E^*) \text{ for } E \geq E^*$$

Where $0 \leq \alpha \leq 1$ and $c>0$.

The incorporation of E* can be justified by accepting public bureaucracy models which assume that the bureaucracy is interested in the expansion of outlays. (Davis, Dempster and Wildasky1966, Niskanen, 1971, Van Dan Doel, 1979, Drakopoulos and Karayiannis, 1999). The kinked indifference curve implies that policy makers change objective when a crucial level of the most important variable is reached. In this specific case when the satisfactory level of employment (E*) is attained, the policy makers care more about the growth perspective. This can be justified in terms of the electoral strategy i.e. giving more weight to a goal because it is perceived to lead to electoral victory.

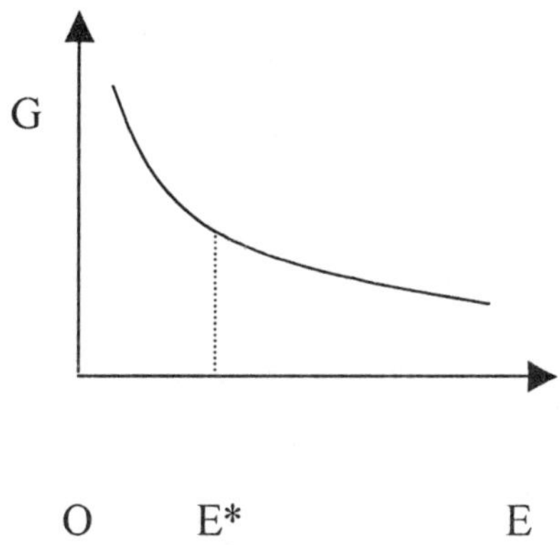

Figure: The policy makers' indifference curve.

2. The West Bengal Experience

In keeping with almost all other States of India, West Bengal still has to absorb most of its labour force in agriculture. But one of the most important achievements of West Bengal Left Front Government, which have been ruling since 1977 at a stretch, is that West Bengal witnessed the third highest position in growth of NSDP agriculture during 1984-85 to 1995-96 (Table 1, prepared from Chand et.ai 2007: Table 6:2531). Agriculture, especially production of food grains, coupled with land reforms and decentralization of rural power has been the most important achievements of Left Front rule in West Bengal. Agricultural production, especially that of rice, grew at a spectacular rate in the state during the 1980s. Part of this is attributed to land reforms itself, to an increase in the incentive to produce more due to transfer of ownership, Patta, or a permanent right given to the cultivator to cultivate land -Barga (Sarkar, 2006). During the 1980s, boro cultivation grew at an annual rate of 12 per cent and overall food grains at a rate of 5.5 per cent. High growth rate in the NSDP agriculture during 1984-85 to 1995-96 helped West Bengal and Punjab to maintain their lead in agricultural

Table 1: Growth in NSDP agriculture in Various States

State	*1984-85 to 1995-96*	*1995-96 to 2004-05*
Rajasthan	5.52	0.30
Chattisgarh		-0.91
Madhya Pradesh (old)	3.63	-0.23
Madhya Pradesh (new)		-0.05
Maharashtra	6.66	0.10
Orissa	-1.18	0.11
Gujarat	5.09	0.48
Karnataka	3.92	0.03
All-India	3.62	1.85
Bihar (new)		2.82
Bihar (old)	-1.71	3.51
Jharkhand		5.39
Andhra Pradesh	3.18	2.69
Uttar Pradesh (new)		1.91
Uttar Pradesh (old)	2.82	1.87
Assam	1.65	0.95
Tamil Nadu	4.95	-1.36
Himachal Pradesh	1.64	3.51
Haryana	4.60	1.98
Jammu and Kashmir	2.18	3.25
Uttaranchal		1.36
West Bengal	4.63	2.67
Punjab	4.00	2.16
Kerala	3.60	-3.54

productivity towards the mid-1990s. But,unfortunately, agricultural growth of West Bengal has been significantly slowed down since the mid 1990s.Except Bihar, Jammu and Kashmir and Himachal Pradesh, all other states showed a deceleration in growth of NSDP agriculture after 1995-96.While West Bengal witnessed a growth rate of 4.63 percent per annum during 1984-85 to 1995-96 - Maharashtra (6.66%),Rajasthan (5.52%),Gujarat (5.09%) and Tamil Nadu (4.95) having higher growth performance than West Bengal - it showed a deceleration in growth of NSDP agriculture during 1995-96 to 2004-05, the performance of West Bengal (2.67%) being lower than Jharkhand (5.39), Himachal Pradesh (3.51), old Bihar (3.51), Jammu and Kashmir (3.25), New Bihar (2.82), and Andhra Pradesh (2.69).(Chand et.al 2007:2531).

As regards industrial sector is concerned, from the early years of the ruling of Left Front Government, the share of West Bengal in all India real value added for organized sector started to decline. The share of West Bengal in all India real value added for organized industries was 11.53% in1981; it went down to 6.43% in 1996-97 (Sarker, 2006:343). The decline of formal sector in West Bengal becomes more prominent if one looks at the growth rates of employment in organized industries— West Bengal (-0.6) along with Bihar (-1.7) and Uttar Pradesh (-0.1) are the states showing negative growth rates in employment for the period 1980-81and 1997-98 among 15 major Indian states (ibid: 343).Table 2 (prepared from Das, 2007, Table 2: 3980) also shows that both output and employment growth in registered industries decelerated during 1970-2002 period in West Bengal.

However, during the post-reform period one may observe a deceleration in growth of NSDP agriculture on the one hand, and lower growth of formal industries on the other in West Bengal. During 1993-2000 periods for the working population as a whole, the growth rate of daily status unemployment per annum for West Bengal (13%) is the highest among 15 major

Table 2: Output and Employment Growth in Registered Industries: 1970-2002

States	*Output Growth*		*Employment Growth*	
	1970-1985	*1986-2002*	*1970-1985*	*1986-2002*
Andhra Pradesh	-0.25	7.28	-3.07	1.91
Assam	3.37	4.91	.45	0.91
Bihar	3.17	-1.04	-2.35	-6.12
Gujarat	4.07	6.95	-1.65	-1.63
Haryana	1.63	5.80	-3.03	-1.29
Himachal Pradesh	7.89	3.96	2.77	-6.59
Jammu and Kashmir	7.67	2.30	2.77	-0.51
Karnataka	3.90	6.71	-0.14	0.33
Kerala	4.63	3.18	-2.30	-1.69
Madhya Pradesh	4.32	5.51	.33	-2.04
Maharashtra	3.30	4.24	-2.37	-1.99
Orissa	4.39	2.69	.59	-2.63
Punjab	6.81	3.55	2.86	-1.76
Rajasthan	3.06	2.72	-0.73	-3.99
Tamil Nadu	2.09	3.12	-2.86	-1.14
Uttar Pradssh	2.66	4.17	-0.64	-3.22
West Bengal	3.30	1.80	-0.58	-2.96
All India	2.93	4.75	-1.41	-1.55

Table 3: Growth Rate of Unemployment, Non-Farm Workers and Wages by States

States	*Unemployment*		*Rural Male Real Wage*		*Rural Real Wage In Manual Agricultural operation (CL)*	
	1993-2003	*1999-2005*	*1993-2003*	*1999-2005*	*1983-1994*	*1994-2000*
Andhra Pradesh	4.9	8.2	4.3	1.5	3	3.6
Assam	0.4	.8	2.4	3.5	2.2	.4
Bihar	4.6	1.5	5.1	3.4	3.2	4.6
Gujarat	-0.8	-1.4	3.4	1.1	1.4	2.9
Haryana	-8.2	12.2	2.8	.8	4	2
Karnataka	-0.3	13.3	3.8	.8	4.1	3.3
Kerala	9.6	6.2	5.5	3.6	1.7	5.9
Madhya Pradesh	7.5	13.7	.9	3.4	4.1	.7
Maharashtra	3.0	10.9	3.1	-.5	3.3	3.2
Orissa	1.1	10.9	1.7	5.9	4.1	1.2
Punjab	7.6	25.7	.2	0	2.6	-.3
Rajasthan	17.8	12.8	3.4	.6	3.2	2.4
Tamil Nadu	0.6	2.3	6.5	0	5.5	4.1
Uttar Pradesh	3.2	4.3	2.9	1.5	3.0	2.1
West Bengal	13 0	-6.5	2.8	.2	4	-2.1

(Contd.)

(Contd. Table 3)

States	*Rural Real Wage In Manual Non-Agricultural operation(CL)*		*Non-farm Worker*	
	1983-1994	*1994-2000*	*19993-2000*	*1999-2005*
Andhra Pradesh	2.5	6.4	0.7	7.1
Assam	2.8	.5	9.9	-0.1
Bihar	4.6	2.8	5.1	7.7
Gujarat	1.9	1.2	0.6	4.5
Haryana	2.2	2.7	1.8	8.6
Karnataka	4.3	5.9	-1.4	3.8
Kerala	3.9	4.9	4.3	3.1
Madhya Pradesh	2.4	2.4	3.7	7.8
Maharashtra	5	4.7	0.0	5.5
Orissa	4.3	3.1	2.0	11.1
Punjab	1.8	2.0	4.4	6.7
Rajasthan	3.1	3.9	1.7	7.1
Tamil Nadu	5.5	7.6	-0.3	1.1
Uttar Pradesh	2.5	2.0	3.7	7.4
West Bengal	4.5	-1.7	-1.0	4.3

Indian states excluding Rajasthan (17.8%). But despite deceleration in the growth of NSDP agriculture and lower growth of formal industries, the employment scenario completely changed during 1999-2005 period. West Bengal show the highest daily status of employment during 1999-2005 periods of the major 15 states, the growth rate of unemployment in West Bengal being -6.5% per annum during 1999-2005 period (Table: 3, prepared from Himanshu, 2007, Table 9:504).

Non-farm employment significantly increased during the period in rural areas. Closer inspection of the data suggests that most of these increase in employment during 1999-2005 was in the form of self employment with days of wage labour actually decreasing (ibid).What is most important is that despite highest growth of employment per annum among 15 major Indian states during 1999-2005 period, the growth rate of rural male real wage per annum (both agricultural and non agricultural workers together) is the lowest (0.2 percent per annum) among the major Indian states excluding Maharashtra.

If one looks back, one may find that real rural male wage in West Bengal decelerated during 1993-2005 period compared with 1983-1994 period.(Srivastava and Singh 2006, Himanshu 2007). Categorically, casual labor of both agricultural and non agricultural operations in the rural areas were more adversely affected for such a deceleration. Between 1993-2000, the growth rate of rural real wage for casual labours (15-59 years) in manual agricultural operation and manual non-agricultural operation were -2.1% and -1.7% per annum respectively and these two figures are the lowest among 15 major Indian states for the same period (Srivastava and Singh 2006: pp. 4055-4056).

Despite such a lower growth rate for rural real wage in both farm and non-farm sectors in rural areas during the long period of ruling of Left Front Government of West Bengal at a stretch, the highest growth rate of employment among major

Indian states made an strong positive impetus on reduction in rural poverty during 1999-2005, the poverty head count ratio from EUS (employment unemployment surveys) being 43.8% and 29.4% during 1999-2000 and 2004-05 respectively (Himanshu, 2007:501). The annual decrease in rural poverty that appears in poverty head count ratio from EUS during 1999-2005, was-2.9%, the 3rd highest annual decrease after Assam (-5.6%) and Bihar (-3.2%). But, significantly, during both the periods (1999-2000 and 2004-05) rural poverty headcount ratio was lower than all India average. Even the relative position of rural poverty headcount ratio of West Bengal from1999-2000 to 2004-05 improve, if not significantly, because during both the periods rural poverty headcount ratio of West Bengal was lower than both most of the 15 major Indian states and national average and rural inequality (calculated from Gini ratio) increased during this period more than most of the major Indian states (ibid: Tables 5 and 3).

3. Conclusion

However the success of left front government's priority policy objectives, particularly in rural West Bengal, for over 31 years of their ruling period is that the proportion of people living below poverty line is not only below all India average but also lower than most of the major Indian states. Not only has the growth rate of real rural wage (both farm and non farm sector) per annum been decelerated substantially during the long period of their journey, but also does the growth of real rural wage in 1999-2005 take the second lowest position after Maharashtra, despite the fact that there was an increase in rural non-farm employment with higher increase in rural inequality than most of the major Indian states. Thus in the process of agriculture-industry interactions, West Bengal Left Front Government have been lying much below the critical level of satisfying their prime-policy objectives during their long period of journey they started in 1977.

Notes

1. Employment generation, increase in income and poverty reduction are the priority-policy objectives which the Left Front Government of West Bengal have been announcing in their budget proposals every year.

References

Baarro, R and Gordon, D. (1983): 'A positive theory of monetary policy in a natural rate model', *Journal of Political Economy*,Vol. 91, 589-610.

Banerjee, P.S. (2008): 'The Party and Panchayats in West Bengal', *Economic and Political Weekly*, Vol. XLIII, No. 24, June 14.

Bhattacharya, D and K. Rana (2008): Politics of PDS Anger in West Bengal, *Economic and Political Weekly*, Vol. XLIII, No. 5, Feb. 2.

Chand, R., S.S. Raju and L.M. Pandey (2007): 'Growth crisis in agriculture: Severity and options in national and state levels', *Economic and Political Weekly*, Vol. LII, No. 26, June 30.

Chatterjee, P. (2009): 'The coming Crisis in West Bengal', *Economic and Political Weekly,* Vol. XLIV, No. 6, Feb. 28.

Das, P. (2007): " Economic Reform, Output and Employment Growth in Manucturing :Testing Kaldor's Hypotheses, *Economic and Political Weekly,* Vol. XLII, No. 39, Sept. 29.

Drakopoulos, S.A. (2004): 'Satisficing and sequential targets in economic policy : A politico Economic approach', *Contribution to Political Economy* ,Vol. 23, 49-64.

Fisher, D. (1968): 'The objective of British monetary policy', 1951-64, *Journal of Finance* , Vol. 23, 821-31.

Gylfason, T. and A. Lindbeck, (1986): 'Endogenous unions and governments', *European Economic Review*, .Vol. 30, 5-26.

Himanshu (2007): 'Recent trends in poverty and Inequality: Some preliminary results', *Economic and Political Weekly*, Vol. XLII, No. 6, Feb. 10.

Kydland, F. and E. Prescott (1977): 'Rules rather than discretion : The inconsistency of optimal plans', *Journal of Political Economy*, Vol. 84,473-91.

Mosley, P. (1976): 'Towards a satisficing theory of economic policy', *Economic Journal*, Vol. 86, 59-72.

Mosley, P. and Cracknell(1984): 'Endogenous government policy in a model of the U.K. economy' , *Applied Economics*.Vol.16, 433-45.

Reserve Bank of India: *'18. State Finance'*, www.tn.gov.in/dear/state 20% fin.pdf.

Sarkar, A. (2006): 'Political Economy of West Bengal: A puzzle and a hypothesis', *Economic and Political Weekly*,Vol. XLI, No. 4, Jan. 28

Srivastava, R. and R. Singh .(2006): ' Rural wages during the 1990s: a re-estimation', *Economic and Political Weekly* Vol. XLI, No. 38, Sept. 23.

Thel, H . (1956): ' On the theory of economic Policy', *American Economic Review*, Vol. 46 (supplement) 360-66.

Tinbergen, J. (1952): *'On the theory of economic policy'* , Amsterdam-North Holland.

Timbergen, J. (1956): *'Economic policy: principles and design'*, Amsterdam-North Holland.

William, Glyn (1999): ' Panchayat raj and the changing micro politics in West Bengal' in Roogaly Ben et al (eds.), *Sonar Bangla*? Sage Publication, New Delhi.

6

Regional Variations in Occupational Segregation in India : Some Evidence from NSS Data

Mousumi Dutta and S. Satyabhama

1. Introduction

Gender based occupational segregation is one of the most important factors contributing to inequality between labour markets around the world. It concerns both the tendency for men and women to be employed in different occupations (horizontal segregation) and the tendency for women and men to be employed in different positions within the same occupation or occupation group (vertical segregation). In a situation where there is extremely detailed occupational classification, these two aspects of occupational segregation become equivalent.

In recent years, the issue of impact of policies of liberalization and globalization on women's pattern of work and subsequently on occupational segregation has gained importance. Specifically there is a debate on the tendency generated by neo-liberal economic policies towards feminisation of workforce (Standing, 1989; 1999). The term, feminisation is used in two senses: first is simply that of an increasing presence of women in the workforce. Evidence shows that female work participation rate rose in a large number of countries, particularly less developed countries, while male work participation rates fell, as did the female share of workforce. Secondly, it was argued that changes in the global structure of production with increasing emphasis on reduction of labour costs through greater labour market flexibility have influenced the gender division of labour. This has resulted in a changing structure of jobs, with typically male jobs being taken up by female workers, and such jobs becoming associated with lower wages, less security and other characteristics of informal employment.

Section 2 addresses several issues related to women workforce participation. Section 3 analyses the trend involved in women employment in India in non-agricultural sector over the recent years and brings out the basic issue of job segregation. Since the rural sector is predominantly agricultural and the issues pertaining to gender division of agricultural tasks are distinct, only urban sectors have been considered for our analysis. We have used the ***size adjusted Duncan index*** to calculate the ***job segregation index*** over the major states in India for two time periods: 1993-94 and 1999-2000. One-digit classification of different types of occupations as per the National Industrial Classification (NIC) has been used to calculate these indices. Regional variations in the segregation index and changes in the value of indices between the two rounds are examined, and interpreted. However, one-digit classification does not provide much information on the specific industries in which women workers are clustered. The importance of undertaking more detailed analysis is highlighted in Section 4 with specific reference to the trends in occupational segregation in West Bengal's manufacturing sector. Section 5 concludes by indicating some policy implications of the study.

2. Women and Work: Some Issues

2.1. Dual Burden and Casualisation

A major finding of the Time Use Surveys across the globe has been that women carry a disproportionately greater burden of work than men and since women are responsible for a greater share of non-SNA (System of National Accounts) work in the care economy (i.e. home-based work which is difficult to measure). They enter the labour market already overburdened with work. A macro level Time Use Survey was conducted in six major States viz. Gujarat, Haryana, Madhya Pradesh, Meghalaya, Orissa and Tamil Nadu during July 1998 to June 1999 by the Central Statistical Organisation covering 18,591 households and taking into account all members of the household aged 6 years and above. According to the Survey, in the production of own-account services which qualify for inclusion in the satellite accounts, on an average a female spent 34.6 hours per week as compared to 3.6 hours spent by a male.

The Female Economic Activity Rate (FEAR)[1] in India is 42 % (Human Development Report, 2001) compared to 55.6 % in Australia, 55 % in Indonesia and 82.9 % in Mozambique. The female to male ratio of participation in economic activity (F/M) is less than 100 in all countries except China. For India the F/M ratio is 50.

Trends in work participation rate in India as per NSSO estimates indicate that the work participation rates across gender in rural and urban areas has registered a sharp decline between 1983 and 1999. The Sectoral profile of female work force indicates that amongst rural women workers, a majority are employed in agriculture as labourers and cultivators. In the urban areas, women workers are primarily employed in the unorganized sectors such as household industries, petty trades and services, buildings and construction etc. As on March 31, 1999, women constituted about 17.2% of the organized sector (both public and private) employment. Though the overall proportion of women's employment to total employment registered an increase of 0.8% as compared to the corresponding proportion of women employed in 1998, it still constitutes a far from satisfactory achievement in desired employment levels. The distribution of women employees across industries reveals that community, social and personnel services sectors employed 55.6% of women workers followed by manufacturing (21.4%) agriculture and allied occupations (9.8%) and finance, insurance, real estate and business (4.9%). In 1997 women workers employed in factories, mines and plantations constituted 14%, 6% and 51% respectively of the total work force.

The distribution of female work participation by status of employment indicates that there is a pronounced declining trend in the importance of the self employed category in both rural and urban areas and an overall increase in the casualisation of the women work force from 31.4 % in 1972-73 to 40.9 % in 1997 in rural India with a marginal decline to 39.6 % in 1999-2000. In

Figure-1: Year-wise Distribution of Employment by Status of Employment

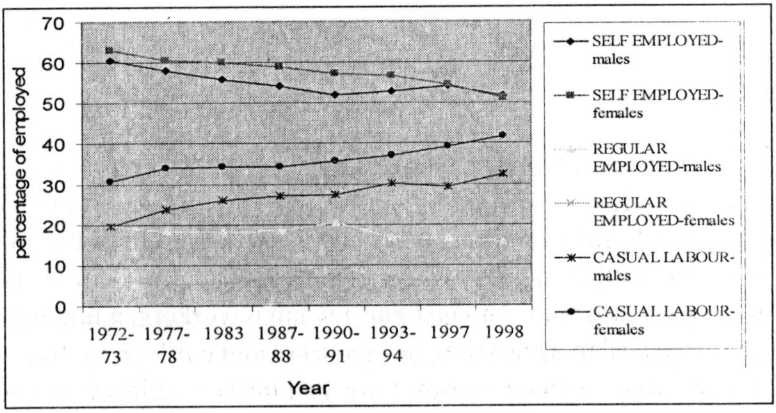

urban India there is a reversal of this trend with an increase in work participation rates of females under regular employment category and a decline in casualisation. Figure 1 gives a summary of overall distribution of employment by status of employment for a time span of more than twenty five years.

The figure reveals the facts that:

- Over the years, the distribution of employment has varied among the three status considered- self employed, regular employed and casual labour.
- Women are concentrated more and more in the informal sector as the percentage of women working as self employed or casual labourers are more as compared to males.
- Female employment has certainly shown an uptrend as far as casual labour is considered (from 30.9% in 1972-73 to 42% in 1998).
- Females working as 'regular employed' are few in number compared to males. This reveals that the percentage of women working in organized sector is low as compared to the number of males. There has been only a marginal increase in the number of female employees in the organized sector (from 6.3% in 1972-73 to 6.9% in 1998).

2.2. Problem of Late Entry

As per the NSSO 55th Round on Employment and Unemployment in India 1999-2000, women tend to enter the labour market later than men. Work participation of males is considerable higher in the age group of 15-29. In rural areas female work participation rate has been the highest at 58.6 % in the age group of 40-44 and is above 50 % in the age group 30-54. In urban areas female work participation rate is highest at 28.5 % in the age group 35-39 and is 28.3 % in age group 40-44. Early marriage and multiple child bearing depress the female work force participation rates in the 15-29 age group. In most developed and developing countries, the age group 15-25 exhibits a peak in women's work force participation rates.

Looking to the requirements for providing a supportive legal framework, the Equal Remuneration Act, 1976, provides for payment of equal remuneration to men and women for work of a similar nature. The Supreme Court in its order dated 13.8.97 has laid down guidelines for the prevention of sexual harassment of women employees at the workplace. In February 1998, an amendment in the Central Civil Services (Conduct) Rules, 1964 has been carried out to give effect to the guidelines. The Ministry of Labour has also amended the Industrial Employment (Standing Orders) Act, 1964, to make the Supreme Court guidelines applicable to private employees. Improvement in the quality of women's employment depends upon increased access to education and skill development training. The Women's Vocational Training Programme was launched by Ministry of Labour in 1974. A separate Women's Cell has also been formed for the purpose and has now developed into the Women's Occupational Training Directorate. Under this Directorate, the institutional network includes a National Vocational Training Institute at Noida and 10 regional Vocational Training Institutes in different parts of the country. There are about 765 Institutes (231 Women Industrial Training Institutes and 534 Women Wings in General Industrial Training Institutes (ITI) /Private ITI with about 46,750 training seats for providing vocational training facilities for women at craftsman level. Statutory provisions have also been made in existing labour laws for organizing child care centers for the benefit of women workers.

In spite of these attempts dual burden of work together with problem of late entry still result in 'gender stereotypes' in occupational structure.

2.3. Issue of Job Segregation

Job segregation refers to the inequality in the concentration of men and women in different occupational categories. The main reasons for studying occupational segregation are to understand the status (both objective and subjective) of women in society, the efficiency of labour market (including labour rigidities), male female wage differentials and several aspects of socio-economic development (including for example, poverty and human development). Among labour economists a large part of the analysis of occupational segregation has focused has contributed to gender differentials in wages and earnings and thus, to inequity in labour market.

There is a large international literature documenting the degree and pattern of occupational segregation by gender, trends in segregation as well as factors contributing to changes in occupation segregation. Generally speaking, among developed countries scholars have observed a tendency for occupational segregation to decline over time. In the process of economic growth, women's work participation has risen and women have entered a wider range of jobs and occupations. The historical experience suggests that gender segregation of occupations is likely to decline with a rise in female work participation. Nevertheless, substantial gender differentials in occupation structure remain even in high income countries.

Occupational segregation by gender negatively affects the efficiency of the labour market. Segregation causes labour market inflexibility because it restrains mobility between male and female occupations. Occupational segregation based on worker's sex also has a negative impact on women, their career opportunities and pay, the quality of their working life and the valuation of their work. Even where women enter traditionally male dominated occupations (industries), they are more likely than men to be found in lower status and lower paid positions. The polarization of labour market by gender also leads to qualitative differences between women's and men's work. Typically, women's work generally involves less decision making and independent planning than does typical men's work; it is also more restricted in space and time and more monotonous. This polarization affects education decision early in life (e.g. choice of field of study) as well as later decisions about which parent will disrupt his/her career to look after children, thereby reinforcing objective reasons for gender inequality in the labour market and perpetuating inequality across generations.

However, gender based occupational segregation also has a positive side for women as it protects some of women's employment from male competition and maintains demand for female labour.

3. Occupational Segregation in Non-Agricultural Sector in Urban India

3.1. Description of Sample

In this section we examine the differences between the distribution of male workers and female workers across non agricultural broad sections of industry in urban India, using data from the NSSO 50th round (1993-94) and 55th round (1999-00). Since data for agriculture sector is not available for 1999-00, we have taken only the non agricultural sector in our analysis.

We have taken the data pertaining to usual status - that is, the activity of person during the reference period of 365 days preceding the date of survey. Further, we have utilized information on both principal usual status workers as well as subsidiary status workers.

The information on the industries is coded in NSSO surveys using the National Industrial Classification (NIC), 1998 system. The data in the 55th round has a wider classification as far as the industry section is concerned. We have excluded them from our analysis for the sake of comparability.

The industry classifications used at the 1-digit level are:

- Mining and quarrying

- Manufacturing
- Electricity
- Construction
- Wholesale and retail trade
- Transport, storage etc
- Financial, insurance and other services
- Community services

3.2. Methodology

Two simple indicators have been used to monitor the share of women in the workforce. These indicators are:

(a) Female work participation rate or labour force participation rate

(b) Female share in total workforce

In the literature on segregation, where the concern has been with detailed occupation, the variable of interest has been the sex ratio or gender ratio of each industry defined as Fi/Mi, where

Fi= female worker in ith industry

Mi= male worker in ith industry.

Alternatively, female representation or the percentage of women workers in an occupation (PFEM) that is, Fi/Ti where Fi and Ti are female and total workers in the ith industry respectively, can be used as an indicator of the degree of feminisation in the industry and thus to examine occupational segregation.

The most commonly used measure of segregation is the ***Duncan and Duncan index*** of Dissimilarity. This is defined as

$$ID = \frac{1}{2} \Sigma \mid Fi/F - Mi/M \mid$$

Where, Fi and Mi are the male and female workers in the i-th occupation and F and M are total male and female workers respectively. The value of the ID ranges from 0 (no segregation) to 1 (total segregation).

The index can be interpreted as the minimum proportion of men plus the minimum proportion of women who would need to change occupation in industry to ensure that the proportion of women workers in all industries is identical and equal to female proportion of labour force. When there is no segregation the share of women in each occupation will be the same as the share of women in the workforce.

The ID has been criticized for being dependent on occupational structure. A size adjusted index, DS that adjusts for the size of each occupation can be defined as

$$DS= \tfrac{1}{2} \Sigma \,|\, \{Fi/Ti/(\Sigma Fi/Ti)\}- \{Mi/Ti/(\Sigma Mi/Ti)\} \,|$$

where Fi and Mi are female and male workers in the ith occupation and Ti are total workers in the ith occupation.

We can further decompose the ID measure into sub-group measures. A change in the value of Duncan index is decomposed into:

(1) Sex- composition effect, and
(2) Occupation Mix effect.

The **sex composition effect** arises from changes in sex composition within occupations holding size of occupations constant. It can be expressed as:

$$= \tfrac{1}{2} [\, \Sigma \,|\, (f_{i2}T_{i1}/\Sigma f_{i2}T_{i1})-(m_{i2}T_{i1}/\Sigma m_{i2}T_{i1}) \,| \\ -\Sigma \,|\, (f_{i1}T_{i1}/\Sigma\, f_{i1}T_{i1})-(m_{i1}T_{i1}/\Sigma m_{i1}T_{i1}) \,|\,]$$

The **occupation mix effect** arises from changes in occupational composition, holding the sex composition of occupations constant. It can be expressed as:

$$=\frac{1}{2}\left[\Sigma \left| (f_{i1}T_{i2}/\Sigma f_{i1}T_{i1})-(m_{i1}T_{i2}/\Sigma m_{i1}T_{i2}) \right| - \Sigma \left| (f_{i1}T_{i1}/\Sigma_{fi1}T_{i1}) - (m_{i1}T_{i1}/\Sigma m_{i1}T_{i1}) \right| \right]$$

where,

f_{it}= percent female in occupation i in time t

m_{it}= percent male in occupation i in time t

T_{it}= total no of workers in occupation i in time t

3.3. Results

In this section we are presenting the picture of occupational segregation for 15 major states in India. Table1 gives the values of the size adjusted Duncan Indices (DS) for the two rounds of NSSO.

Table-1: Comparison of segregation using size adjusted Duncan Index

State	*DS(93-94)*	*DS(99- 00)*
Andhra Pradesh	0.48	0.47
Assam	0.76	0.71
Bihar	0.64	0.37
Gujarat	0.72	0.40
Haryana	0.53	0.06
Karnataka	0.49	0.35
Kerala	0.66	0.40
Madhya Pradesh	0.52	0.43
Maharashtra	0.70	0.42
Orissa	0.55	0.22
Punjab	0.79	0.14
Rajasthan	0.46	0.58
Tamil Nadu	0.53	0.26
Uttar Pradesh	0.49	0.31
West Bengal	0.79	0.23

We know that the closer the value of Duncan Index is to unity, the greater will be the extent of segregation. Hence the segregation was highest in Punjab and West Bengal in 93-94, followed by Assam, Gujarat and Maharashtra. It was lowest in Rajasthan, followed by Andhra Pradesh, Karnataka and Uttar Pradesh. During 1999-2000 the segregation decreases almost for all states, except for Rajasthan where the value of index rose to 0.58 from 0.46. Further we find that except Assam, the index has come down to 0.5 or less for all states. An interesting thing in this context is to note that while extent of segregation is higher in northern and western states like Maharashtra, Gujarat and Punjab in 1993-94 it is moderate to low in the four major states of south India. One of the reasons for this may be the cultural practices that vary from region to region. It is generally said that north India is more patriarchal and feudal than south India. Women in northern India have more restrictions placed on their behavior, thereby restricting their access to work. Southern India tends to be more egalitarian, women have relatively more freedom, and women have a more prominent presence in society.

West Bengal shows an interesting pattern in the comparison of job segregation in the two time points. In 1993-94, the degree of job segregation was high (0.79) whereas in 1999-2000 the Duncan Index fell to 0.23.

To analyze whether the decrease in job segregation is indeed due to rise in labour force participation rates or not we regress the calculated Duncan Index on the labour force participation rates for both years.

The regression results are presented in Table-2 and Table-3.

The regression results interestingly suggest that the effect of labour force participation rates on the size adjusted Duncan

Table-2: Regression of size adjusted Duncan Index on LFPR (93-94)

Regression Statistics	
Multiple R	0.266046
R Square	0.07078
Adjusted R Square	-0.0007
Standard Error	0.120071
Observations	15

ANOVA

	df	*SS*	*MS*	*F*
Regression	1	0.014276	0.014276	0.990232
Residual	13	0.187422	0.014417	
Total	14	0.201698		

	Coefficients	*Standard Error*	*t Stat*	*P-value*	*Lower 95%*	*Upper 95%*
Intercept	0.710986	0.108311	6.564297	1.81E-05	0.476994	0.944978
LFPR	-0.00064	0.000644	-0.9951	0.337848	-0.00203	0.00075

Table-3: Regression of size adjusted Duncan Index on LFPR (99-00)

Regression Statistics	
Multiple R	0.141359
R Square	0.019982
Adjusted R Square	-0.0554
Standard Error	0.169687
Observations	15

ANOVA				
	df	*SS*	*MS*	*F*
Regression	1	0.007632	0.007632	0.265067
Residual	13	0.37432	0.028794	
Total	14	0.381952		

	Coefficients	*Standard Error*	*t Stat*	*P-value*	*Lower 95%*	*Upper 95%*
Intercept	0.282758	0.151478	1.866667	0.084662	-0.04449	0.610005
LFPR	0.0005	0.000971	0.514847	0.615301	-0.0016	0.002598

index is not significant for both the years implying that there is actually no significant effect of the rising work participation among women on gender segregation across industries. This may be attributed to the rising labour costs which may have influenced the gender division of labour. Women tend to be employed as contract employers and have no power as such in the union.

In the next section we are shifting our focus on a particular sector of a particular state. Using 3-digit NIC code we have examined the occupational segregation in manufacturing sector in West Bengal.

4. Occupational Segregation in Manufacturing Sector of West Bengal

As far as the structure of manufacturing sector of West Bengal is concerned, it can be observed that this sector is dominated by very small type of enterprises known as Own Account Manufacturing Enterprises (OAMEs). Within manufacturing, the basic problem seems to be that much of the growth has come from large units which are less employment-intensive whereas many of the labour-using small units have eventually closed down.

4.1. Pattern of Segregation

We have attempted to classify the manufacturing industry in West Bengal under the 3-digit classification based on the patterns of job segregation and tried to find whether the industries are male dominated or female dominated using the concept of PFEM.

The broad description of the industries considered for the analysis is given in Table-I in the Appendix.

We are using four categories, namely Male Dominated, Female Under represented, Female Dominated, Female Over represented, to indicate continuous improvement of female participation in work force. The results are as follows:

Table-4: Classification of Industries based on PFEM

3 digits Ind code (NIC) (manufacturing)	*Classification (1993-94)*	*Classification (1999-00)*
151	Male Dominated	Male Dominated
153	Male Dominated	Female Under-Represented
154	Male Dominated	Male Dominated
155	Male Dominated	Male Dominated
160	Female Dominated	Female Over Represented
171	Male Dominated	Male Dominated
172	Male Dominated	Female Under-Represented
181	Male Dominated	Male Dominated
192	Male Dominated	Male Dominated
202	Female Over represented	Female Under-Represented
210	Male Dominated	Male Dominated
221	Male Dominated	Female Under-Represented
222	Male Dominated	Male Dominated
231	Male Dominated	Male Dominated
241	Male Dominated	Female Under-Represented
242	Female Over Represented	Male Dominated
251	Male Dominated	Male Dominated
252	Male Dominated	Male Dominated
269	Female Under-Represented	Male Dominated
271	Male Dominated	Male Dominated
272	Male Dominated	Male Dominated
281	Male Dominated	Male Dominated
289	Male Dominated	Male Dominated
291	Male Dominated	Male Dominated
292	Female Over Represented	Male Dominated
293	Male Dominated	Male Dominated

(Contd.)

(Contd. Table 4)

3 digits Ind code (NIC) (manufacturing)	*Classification (1993-94)*	*Classification (1999-00)*
311	Male Dominated	Male Dominated
312	Male Dominated	Male Dominated
353	Male Dominated	Male Dominated
361	Male Dominated	Male Dominated
369	Male Dominated	Male Dominated

Table 4 reveals that

- The major 3 digit industries used in the analysis are male dominated. In 1993-94 only in five industries among thirty one, namely, manufacturing of tobacco and tobacco related products; canning and preservation of fruits and vegetables; wool spinning weaving and processing in mills; manufacture of textiles/textile products not elsewhere classified like linoleum, padding wadding, upholstering filling etc.; and manufacturing of wearing apparel of leather and substitutes of leather (being coded as 160, 202, 242, 269, 292 respectively) female are well represented. In 1999-2000 the figure rises to six. The industries showing visible female participation are mining of ceramic, refractory and glass minerals; manufacturing of tobacco and tobacco related products; manufacturing of curtain, bedcover and furnishing; canning and preservation of fruits and vegetables; manufacture of wines; wool spinning weaving and processing other than in mill (being coded as 153, 160, 172, 202, 221, 241 respectively).

- The single industry, namely, manufacturing of tobacco and tobacco related products (code 160) was female dominated in 1993-94. Over time, the proportion of female workers has increased so that female workers have become over represented.

- Manufacture of curtain, bedcover and furnishing (code172) shows an 'improvement' from being male dominated to being a sector where female workers are under represented.

- Canning and preservation of fruits and vegetables (code 202) has predominantly been a female industry. However the female participation in that industry has decreased so that it has become a sector where female workers are under represented.

- Wool spinning weaving and processing in mills (code 242) had been a female over represented industry in 1993-94 whereas it became male dominated in 1999-00. A similar situation was observed for category 292 (manufacturing of wearing apparel of leather and substitutes of leather).

- Conversely industry 241(wool spinning weaving and processing other than in mills became a female under represented sector in 1999-00 from male dominated resulting from an increase influx of female labour in the unorganized sector.

4.2. Is there an Occupation Pyramid?

Even among occupations where women are well represented, it has been argued that there is a hierarchy of occupations with a tendency for women to be concentrated in the lower rungs of the hierarchy. In other words, it is argued that within a given sector, there is job pyramid and women tend to be assigned to jobs that require limited skills and education, that pay low wages with less scope for career advancement. This tendency is not very easy to explain with data on industries alone (that is, without information on earnings, job description etc.).

Nevertheless, we can observe some clear patterns of hierarchy even in occupations with a significant representation of women. As is observed, most women tend to be concentrated in small scale industries preparing *vanaspati ghee*, canning and preserving of fruits and vegetables. Spinning and Weaving are other sectors traditionally dominated by female workers. But as these sectors become organized, women are being increasingly displaced by their male counterparts.

4.3. Index of Dissimilarity and Size Adjusted Duncan Index

The Duncan Index of Dissimilarity (ID) and the size adjusted Duncan index (DS) show different trends for the manufacturing sector in West Bengal, at the 3 digit level. We have already seen that the size adjusted index of dissimilarity has declined considerably for West Bengal implying a decline in job segregation. The 3-digit analysis shows the same trend. As is evident from the segregation curves and the summary tables there has been a decline in the number of male dominated industries. This is clearly being reflected in the size adjusted Duncan index.

Table-5: Segregation Indices

Index	*1993-94*	*1999-00*
Index of dissimilarity (ID)	0.34	0.38
Duncan index (DS)	0.61	0.55

The index of Dissimilarity (ID) is expected to show no segregation when there is a perfect correspondence between the sex ratio within each occupation and the overall rate of female work participation. Since the overall female work participation rate in India as a whole and West Bengal in particular is low this is not a very good measure for comparing segregation across states. However, we have attempted to decompose changes in segregation at the 3-digit level, as measured by the Dissimilarity Index (ID) into the sex composition effect and the occupation mix effect. Both the effect for our analysis turns out to be positive (Sex Composition Effect = 0.0539 and Occupation Mix Effect = 0.1305). Both the effects can be said to contribute to a rise in occupational segregation. In other words, the increase in segregation was caused by both a change in the gender ratio along with a change in the structure of labour force.

4.4. Segregation and Inequality

As occupation segregation is concerned with inequality in the distribution of men and women across occupations, many scholars have applied the concepts used for measurement of income inequality to the measurement of segregation. As Duetsh, Fluckiger and Silber (1994) argue, "the gender ratio in each occupation plays the role of individual income". Thus, one can generate segregation curves, similar to Lorenz curves, by ranking all occupations in ascending order of gender ratio (Fi/Mi). The segregation curve therefore represents a cumulative fraction of males on the abscissa and of females on the ordinate (Hutchens, 1991).

As in the case of Lorenz curves a complete ranking of two distributions is possible only if the segregation curves for the two time periods do not intersect. However, if the segregation curves crosses, different indices of segregation can give different rankings so value judgments will have to be used in choosing the measure.

The plot of the segregation curves for 1993-94 and 1999-00 (Fig. 2) reveals that the curves coincide for low values, while they intersect twice at higher values. This implies that an unambiguous conclusion about changes in segregation is very difficult to be inferred. For low values, there is no change in the segregation curve and both the years show similar pattern. The maximum change is observed for high values only.

In case of women employment, a concentrated pattern is observed in the industrial distribution of women workers. Most

Figure-2: The Segregation Curve

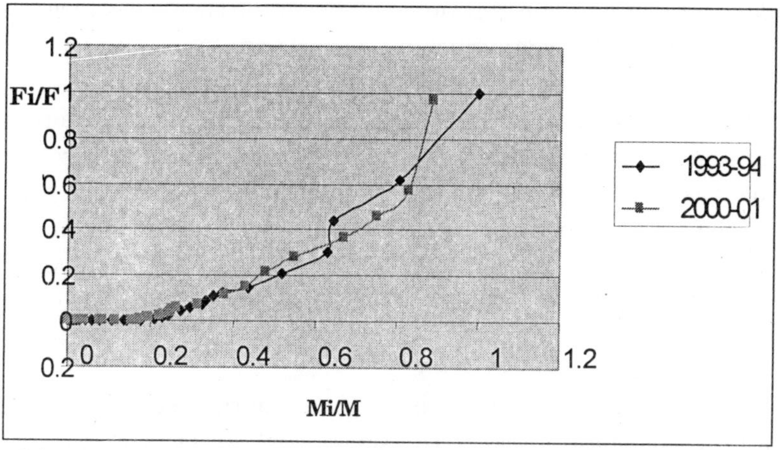

of the industries which show female dominance show a contract employment pattern. One of the major industries having contract employment, tobacco products, is dominated by female workers. Spinning, weaving and finishing of textiles as well as canning and preservation of fruits and vegetables are other low technology industries which are found to be major employers of contract workers. Interestingly all these industries show some form of female dominance. It has been observed that the use of contract relative to regular workers has grown significantly over the two time periods for most of the individual industries. The industry groups such as tobacco products and manufacturing of meat, fish, fruit, vegetables and oils have in particular generated more jobs for female- contract driven workers.

5. Conclusion

The study reveals that most significant feature of the labour force in India is a low rate of female labour force participation. Associated with this is a low share of women in the workforce. Although there has been a gradual rise in the share of women in the total non-agricultural workforce, the measures of segregation do not point any tendency towards feminisation of labour in the 1990s.

In case of manufacturing industry in West Bengal while the Duncan and Duncan Index of dissimilarity shows a rise in segregation, the Size Adjusted Dissimilarity Index shows a fall in value for data on 3- digit level. A decomposition of the Duncan Index shows that the rise in value was on account of both a change in gender ratio of occupations as well as changes in occupation structure. The rise in value of ID over the two time periods is however, rather small. The segregation curves (similar to Lorenz curves) for 1993 and 2000 considered have intersected, making it difficult to draw a clear conclusion about change in segregation.

In conclusion, there is need for more research on the factors associated with the observed patterns of gender segregation, and in particular, on barriers to female employment. Although increased educational attainment does open up new occupational avenues for women, the level of educational attainment among women workers still remains low, as does overall participation in the labour market. Thus, in the Indian context, it is important to identify constraints to participation in labour market (such as from the drudgery of domestic work) alongside barriers to entry into specific industries.

APPENDIX

Table I: Description of NIC Codes

NIC Codes	*Description*
151	Mining/quarrying of sand-stone and other building / construction materials of mineral / rock origin, n.e.c.
153	Mining of ceramic, refractory and glass minerals
154	Salt mining/quarrying and screening, etc.
155	Mining of mica
160	Manufacturing of tobacco and tobacco related products
171	Preparation and spinning of cotton fibre including blended cotton

(Contd.)

(Contd. Appendix)

NIC Codes	*Description*
172	Manufacturing of Curtain, Bedcover and Furnishing
181	Manufacturing of all types of textile garments and clothing accessories
192	Manufacturing of leather footwear (excluding repair) except of moulded rubber or plastic.
202	Canning and preservation of fruits and vegetables
210	Manufacture of hydrogenated oils and vanaspati ghee etc.
221	Manufacture of wines
222	Manufacture of malt liquors and malt
231	Cotton spinning other than in mills (charkha)
241	Wool spinning, weaving and finishing other than in mills
242	Wool spinning, weaving and processing in mills
251	Preparatory operations (including carding and combing) on jute and mesta fibres
252	Preparatory operations (including carding and combing) on coir fibres
269	Manufacture of textiles/textile products not elsewhere classified like linoleum, padding wadding, upholstering filling etc.
271	Manufacture of vaneer sheets, plywood and their products
272	Manufacture of structural wooden goods (including treated timber)
281	Manufacture of containers and boxes of paper or paper board
289	Printing and allied activities not elsewhere classified
291	Manufacture of footwear excluding repair
292	Manufacture of wearing apparel of leather and substitutes of leather
293	Manufacture of consumer goods of leather and substitutes of leather; other than apparel and footwear
311	Manufacture of footwear made primarily of vulcanised or moulded rubber and plastics.
312	Manufacture of rubber products not elsewhere classified

(Contd.)

(Contd. Appendix)

NIC Codes	*Description*
353	Manufacture of industrial machinery for food and textile industries
361	Manufacture of insulated wires and cables, including manufacture of optical fibre cables
369	Manufacture of radiographic X-ray apparatus X-ray tubes and parts and manufacture of electrical equipment n.e.c.

References

Anker, Richard (1998), *Gender and jobs, Sex Segregation of Occupations in the World*, International Labour Office, Geneva.

Deutsch, Joseph; Fluckiger, Yves and Silber, Jacques (1994) *"Measuring Occupational Segregation", Journal of Econometrics,* Vol. 61, pp. 133-46.

Hutchens, Robert M. (1991), *"Segregation Curve, Lorenz Curve and Inequality in the Distribution of People across Occupations", Mathematical Social Sciences,* Vol. 21.

Loutfi, Martha Fetherolf (2001), *"Women, gender and work: What is Equality, and how do we get there?", ILO, Geneva.*

Pradhan, Jaya Prakash, *" Trade, Foreign Investment, Technology and Employment Patterns", Indian Journal of Labour Economics,* Vol. 49.

Raychoudhury, Ajitava and Tuhin.K , *"West Bengal economy- Some Contemporary Issues"*.

Standing, Guy (1989), *"Global Feminisation through Flexible Labour", World Development,* Vol. 17.

Swaminathan, Madhura and Majumdar, Sharmila, " Workers in urban India- Changes in Gender segregation of occupations", *Indian Journal of Labour Economics,* Vol. 49.

References

1. The Female Economic Activity Rate (FEAR) is the proportion of female population aged 15 years and above who furnish or are available to furnish, the supply of labour for production of goods and services in accordance with SNA.

7

The Nexus Between Agricultural Prices and Industrial Prices in India : A Time Series Study

Rajnarayan Gupta

I. Introduction

Inflation is a social evil. It is undesirable for any society at any point of time. The policy makers always keep vigil on it and take action to control it whenever it exceeds certain tolerable limit. In order to correct inflation, however, it is necessary to identify its sources. Sometimes, inflation occurs due to price rise in the agricultural sector. Food price hike, for instance is reflected more in the Consumer Price Index (CPI) than in the Wholesale Price index (WPI) and causes misery for the general people. Sometimes, on the other hand, the price level is triggered by manufactured goods. The price rise in the agricultural sector or the manufacturing sector, again, may be due to demand-pull factors or cost-push factors. Remedial measures should be prescribed accordingly.

In India, however, inflation is measured in terms of Wholesale Price Index (WPI) while internationally accepted index for the purpose is Consumer Price Index (CPI). In WPI, primary articles (including agricultural products and minerals) have the weight 22.025 of which the weight of the agricultural goods (food and non-food articles) is 21.540 and that of the minerals is 0.485. The weight of the manufactured products is 63.749 and that of fuel, power, light and lubricants, the third category, is 14.226. The mere weight of a category of products in the index, however, does not represent their true influence on the overall price level. Prices of agricultural goods (food and non-food articles), for instance, can affect manufactured goods' prices. Similarly, manufactured goods' prices can also affect agricultural prices. The intersectoral causality in prices appears important in this context.

Agriculture and industry are interdependent in various ways. Agricultural and industrial prices, for that reason, are likely to be correlated. Agricultural prices, for instance, may affect industrial prices at least in two ways. First, agriculture provides wage goods to the industry. The rise in the prices of agricultural goods and specifically the prices of food articles increases the cost of production and hence the price level in the industrial sector. This is particularly true for the organized industrial sector where wages are indexed for inflation on the basis of CPI which is highly sensitive to the prices of food articles. Even where wage indexation in not practiced he changes in the prices of wage goods must affect wage rate and hence the cost of production. Second, agriculture provides raw materials to industries. Agriculture supplies, for instance, sugarcane to the sugar industry, or raw cotton to the cotton industry or raw jute to the jute industry. The prices of those raw materials are also expected to have some bearing on the prices of finished goods.

As against the flows of wage goods and raw materials from the agricultural sector to the industrial sector there are counter flows as well. Industry provides machineries and instruments as inputs to the farm sector. Agriculture in India is much more mechanized today than earlier. Farmers use pump-sets, tractors, other machineries along with fertilizer and pesticides which are produced in the industrial sector. The industrial goods' prices should therefore have considerable influence on the agricultural prices.

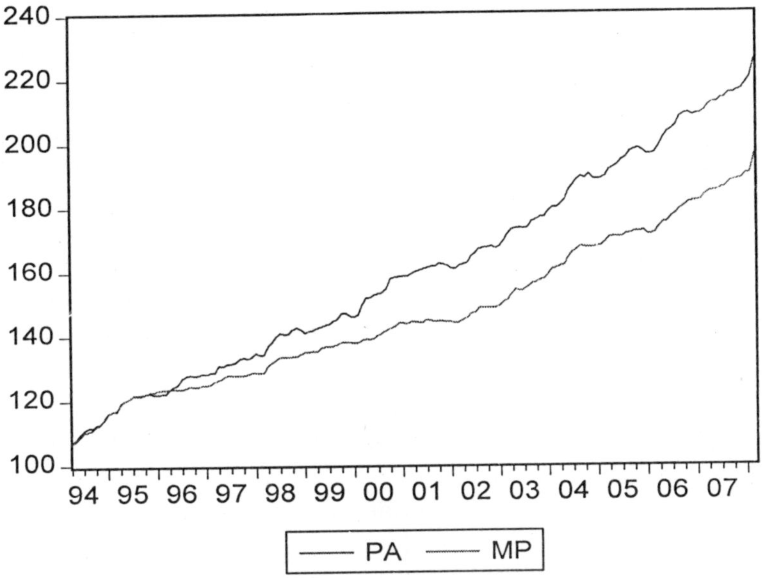

Source : RBI Handbook of Statistics on Indian economy.

Fig. 1 Prices of Primary Articles (PA) and Manufactured Products (MP)

It seems therefore that there is considerable linkage between agricultural prices and industrial prices. The present study attempts to examine the causality between the two. The study contains four sections. Section II describes the methodology and data sources. Section III interprets the empirical findings. The study is concluded in section IV.

II. Methodology and Data Sources

The objective of the study is to investigate the causal relationship between the prices of primary articles (PA) and the prices of manufactured products (MP). Cointegration test appears urgent to explore the long run relationship between the variables. The Engel – Granger two step method has been deployed for that purpose. Cointegration test applies only when the variables are non-stationary but integrated of the same order. The test for cointegration therefore requires the pre-test of stationarity. The stationarity of the variables has been checked with the ADF (Augmented Dickey Fuller) test. The results of the cointegration test suggests further proceedings. If, the variables are cointegrated, then the causality can be tested with the Vector Error Correction (VEC) method, otherwise, unrestricted VAR (Vector Auto Regression) method is suggested.

Data on the prices of primary articles and manufactured products are obtained from the RBI (Reserve Bank of India) Handbook of Statistics on Indian Economy, 2007-08. Monthly data on the two variables for the period from April, 1994 to March, 2008 have been considered for the empirical investigation. The period has been chosen in order to remain confined to the liberalized regime. Availability of data has also guided the choice. In India, inflation is calculated from the WPI data published by RBI. RBI publishes WPI data on (i) all commodities, (ii) primary articles, (iii) food articles, (iv) non-food articles, (v) fuel, power, light and lubricants and (vi) manufactured products. The indices for the period under consideration have their base year 1993-94. In this study, both the variables, viz., MP and PA have been transformed into natural logarithms to minimize the scale effect. lnmp denotes the logarithm of the price index for manufactured products and lnpa denotes the logarithm of the price index for primary articles.

III. Empirical Findings

The results of unit root test are presented in Table I. Results show that both lnmp and lnpa are non-stationary at levels, but stationary at first differences. In other words, lnmp and lnpa are integrated of the same order; both are I(1) variables. It suggests us to run cointegration test. Cointegration has been tested with the Engle – Granger method which requires test for unit root of the residuals (e_t) from the cointegrating equation

$$\ln mp_t = \alpha_0 + \alpha_1 \ln pa_t + u_t \quad \text{...(1)}$$

where u_t is the disturbance term.

However, the ADF test shows that e_t is nonstationary as the value of the ADF test statistic is -1.1864 which is insignificant even at 10 % level. It appears therefore that there is no long run relationship between the prices of primary articles and the prices of manufactured products. In absence of cointegration, error correction model can not be formulated. Instead, it is imperative to apply unrestricted VAR method in order to examine short run causality between the variables. The VAR is formulated as follows.

$$\ln mp_t = \beta + \sum_{i=1}^{k} \delta_i \ln mp_{t-i} + \sum_{j=1}^{l} \gamma_j \ln pa_{t-j} + \zeta_t \text{..........} \quad \text{...(2)}$$

$$\ln pa_t = \beta + \sum_{i=1}^{k} \Phi_i \ln mp_{t-i} + \sum_{j=1}^{l} \mu_j \ln pa_{t-j} + \varepsilon_t \quad \text{....(3)}$$

where ζ_t and ε_t are the two stochastic error terms.

Application of OLS (Ordinary Least Squares) to (2) and (3) produces results which are exhibited in Table II. The appropriate

Table I
Unit Root Test

Variable	*ADF*
lnmp	5.56
Dlnmp	-8.7952*
lnpa	-3.0453
Dlnpa	-9.6002*

Note : * indicates significant at 1% level
D indicates first difference

Table II
VAR Results

Dependent Variable : lnmp		*Dependent Variable : lnpa*	
Regressors	*Coefficients*	*Regressors*	*Coefficients*
$lnmp_{t-1}$	1.21*	$lnmp_{t-1}$	0.22
$lnmp_{t-2}$	-0.19	$lnmp_{t-2}$	0.07
$lnmp_{t-3}$	0.07	$lnmp_{t-3}$	-0.01
$lnmp_{t-4}$	0.00	$lnmp_{t-4}$	-0.19
$lnmp_{t-5}$	-0.11	$lnmp_{t-5}$	0.08
$lnmp_{t-6}$	0.17	$lnmp_{t-6}$	-0.04
$lnmp_{t-7}$	-0.14	$lnmp_{t-7}$	-0.06
$lnmp_{t-8}$	-0.12	$lnmp_{t-8}$	-0.27
$lnmp_{t-9}$	0.20	$lnmp_{t-9}$	0.32
$lnmp_{t-10}$	-0.16	$lnmp_{t-10}$	-0.02
$lnmp_{t-11}$	0.08	$lnmp_{t-11}$	-0.21
$lnmp_{t-12}$	0.01	$lnmp_{t-12}$	0.19
$lnpa_{t-1}$	0.10	$lnpa_{t-1}$	1.09*

(Contd.)

(Contd. Table II)

Dependent Variable : lnmp		*Dependent Variable : lnpa*	
Regressors	*Coefficients*	*Regressors*	*Coefficients*
$lnpa_{t-2}$	-0.09	$lnpa_{t-2}$	-0.27
$lnpa_{t-3}$	-0.01	$lnpa_{t-3}$	-0.00
$lnpa_{t-4}$	-0.18	$lnpa_{t-4}$	-0.09
$lnpa_{t-5}$	0.21	$lnpa_{t-5}$	0.19
$lnpa_{t-6}$	-0.00	$lnpa_{t-6}$	-0.04
$lnpa_{t-7}$	-0.06	$lnpa_{t-7}$	0.06
$lnpa_{t-8}$	0.08	$lnpa_{t-8}$	-0.10
$lnpa_{t-9}$	0.00	$lnpa_{t-9}$	0.09
$lnpa_{t-10}$	0.04	$lnpa_{t-10}$	0.05
$lnpa_{t-11}$	-0.05	$lnpa_{t-11}$	-0.04
$lnpa_{t-12}$	-0.03	$lnpa_{t-12}$	0.01
Constant	-0.02	Constant	-0.06

Note : * indicates significant at 1% level.

lag length has been selected on the basis of Akaike Information Criterion (AIC) and Schwarz Baysian Criterion (SBC). However, VAR results do not indicate causality either running from lnpa to lnmp or the reverse; none of the γ_js and Φ_is are statistically significant at 1% or 5% level.

IV. Conclusion

The empirical results find no evidence of long run relationship between the prices of primary articles and manufactured products. The estimation of the VAR model shows further that there is no causality between them. Thus, in spite of considerable linkage between the two sectors, prices are not interlinked. Agricultural prices and industrial prices move independently, neither of them having significant influence on the other. It casts doubt on the role of cost in determining price. Agriculture supplies wage goods and raw materials to the industry and industry provides agricultural inputs. The price hike in one sector should increase the cost of production in the other. The increase in cost of production, however, does not have substantial effect on prices.

References

Balakrishna, P(1991), *Pricing and Inflation in India*, Oxford University Press.

Enders, W (2004), *Applied Econometric Time Series*, John Wiley & Sons.

Gujarati, D. N. (2003), *Basic Econometrics*, Mc Graw Hill.

Handbook of Statistics on Indian Economy (2007-08), RBI.

Hess,G. D. and Schweitzer, M.E. (2000), "Does Wage Inflation Cause Price Inflation?", Working Paper Series, *Social Science Research Network*.

Kannan, R (1999), 'Inflation Targeting Issues and Relevance for India', *Economic and Political Weekly*, January, 16-23.

Rakshit, Mihir (2007), 'Inflation in Developing Economy-Theory and Policy', *Money and Finance*, September.

RBI Bulletin, various issues.

8

The Interaction between Agriculture and Industry: With Reference to the Current Indian Scenario

Amitava Chatterjee

It is a well-known established empirical find that has been stressed upon by Kuznets and other economists that when a country has rapid economic growth, it is its industrial sector that contributes most to the process. Whether it be capitalistic or socialistic, any country has to quickly develop its industrial sector and its infrastructure if it wants to grow at a fast pace. Take the case of the industrial revolution in England, or in the USA after the Civil War, or even the Soviet Union, after the Bolshevik Revolution and adoption of the Five Year Plans, Rostow has repeatedly emphasized the role of industry in the so-called "take-off" into self-sustained growth and Marx has also stressed upon the growth of a modern industrial sector under the aegis of the capitalist framework.

We must also be aware of the theories of Balanced Growth, particularly the fourth and most extended version of the theory where the question of balance between agriculture and industry has been stressed. This also calls for coordination of these two major sectors in an economy via a benevolent and commanding state Agriculture will be very important in providing the major raw materials and wage goods for the industrial sector. Further, unless the agricultural sector itself has major increase in real income, where will the demand for the merging industrial sector come from? Hence, it will be wrong for the pleasures to neglect the development of the agricultural sector of the economy. It must be remembered that even now 70% of the population of modern India are located in the villages and are part of the agricultural sector in the economy.

What are the recent features of economic growth in India? Though the economy has been growing from about 2005 at about 8% p.a. (which one is of the highest rates of growth in the world next only to China), the growth rate of agriculture has been lagging behind at less than 4% p.a. It is the contribution of industry and the service sector that has pulled up the rate of growth of the economy. This is fully consistent with Kuznet's thesis. Further, the Government has been tinkering with the laws with regard to Special Economic Zones (SEZ) to give a much freer play to industry and has been trying all possible avenues to attract Foreign Portfolio and Direct Investment into India. The different states within India have been engaged in unseemly competition among themselves to attract foreign investment.

Since it is the responsibility of the democratic Government to ensure growth as well as welfare of the majority of people of the country, a very strict vigil is required in all such policies. There is also a question of how much employment will be generated in the new industrial projects and what will be the level of displacement of the agriculturists from their land. There are the other related questions of skill-formation for industry and finally the matter of intergenerational equity in employment and income. One will have to be very careful in judging and balancing the social benefits and costs of all these emerging industrial projects before taking decisions on them. Objectivity and empirical correctness is all-important and must never be sacrificed for other motives which are unrelated to economic issues.

Finally, on this issue of social benefit and costs of these projects particularly in the SEZ's, the question of defining properly the social welfare function and evaluating the weightage of the efficiency factors and equity factors will be crucial in taking a final decision. Interpersonal comparisons of utility cannot really be avoided and messes up matters particularly in a scenario that involves externalities in production and consumption, and leads to intergenerational equity issues because many of the projects require a long gestation lag and give benefits spread over a long period of time.

9

Economic Development in the Shadows of Socio-political Conflicts: An Agenda for West Bengal

Abhijit Dutta

In this article I have attempted to unify strings of theories analyzing Economic Development and socio-political theories analyzing Social Structures and Institutions. Crucial link in these bits of chains, in my perception, is that of Conflict – viewed either from socio-political or from economic angle. There is a long lineage of theoretical postulates mostly from socio-political perspective offering diverse analytical methods, though the economic perspective is also gaining its momentum with a new set of theoretical analysis. The present state of tension and strain visibly operative in different domains of social, political and economic sphere in West Bengal may be put under the microscope of the conflict theory. In the end I have suggested a scheme of empirical testing for verifying these issues.

The notion of Economic Development (often interpreted synonymously with Industrialization) has close association with the modernization theory. Two such perspectives are widely discussed – W.W. Rostow (The Stages of Economic Growth: A Non-Communist Manifesto, 1960) and N. Smelser (Mechanisms of and Adjustments to Change, 1969) – where attempts were made to provide more general perspectives. For Rostow, the processes of change were linear. He suggested: 'all societies can be placed in one of five categories or stages of economic growth'. On the other hand, Smelser was more concerned with the impact of economic development on social structures.

Modernization Theory has two unique but interrelated theoretical supports: *The Classical Evolutionary Theory* (Comte et al) and the *Functionalist Theory* (Talcott Parsons, 1951). The classical evolutionary theory suggested an evolutionary process of transformation and claimed that the social transformation as a unidirectional – from a primitive to an advanced state – process of human evolution. Pragmatically, the transformation is good because it represents progress of human civilization. The rate of change is slow, gradual and piecemeal. Most importantly, social change, in accordance with Darwinian approach to biological development, was evolutionary, not revolutionary. From this angle, traditional societies are built upon social relationships which tend to be face-to-face, personal and familial; hence, act as a constraint on the process of developing efficient production relations in a market. In contrast, modern societies are typically composed of social relationships that are neutral-impersonal, detached and indirect; which makes way for efficient market relationships.

The other school, namely the Functionalism, or its related theories of *Structural-Functionalism* and *Systems Theory* had the following system of belief: human society is like a biological organism, with different parts corresponding to the different institutions that make up a society; each institution performs a specific function for the benefit of the whole. Society is made up of different institutions such as economy, education, family, religion, and legal system. There are four key functions that every institution must perform to maintain the social structure. Parsons points out them as – adaptation by the economy (A), goal attainment by the government (G), integration or linking the institutions together (I) and latency (L): which means maintenance and transmission of values from generation to generation – performed by the family (as a basic human organization), and education. These are known as the AGIL scheme introduced by Parsons. They have tried to identify the set of necessary 'functions' that must be carried out in any society to cope with its environment and achieve its goals, and locate the 'structures' (political parties, socializing agencies, family, etc.) which facilitate the functioning. The theory states that societies tend towards harmony, stability, equilibrium and the status quo. Any behaviour upsetting these conditions will be considered anti-social and therefore punishable.

Socio-economic conflict appears when one or more sectors in the 'balancing chain', i.e. family - civil society - the state etc. fails to perform its functions. The social conflicts are the result of lack of integration among the 'differentiated structures'. The disturbances might take the form of peaceful agitation, political violence, nationalism, revolution and guerrilla warfare. It is interesting to notice that in the bureaucratic socialist state equivalent to the crude notion of 'Stalinist state' first in the former Soviet Union, and then in People's Republic of China, the same notional framework was at work except that the state enjoyed the multi-status of civil society and family.

To analyze social structures and institutions of the society another theoretical approach, namely, *Conflict Theory* has been proposed in contrast with structural functionalism. There are several doctrines of conflict theory which stands different from structural functionalism. Conflict theorists like Ralf Dahrendorf

(1959) view society as a composite entity consisting of organizations such as the state, a religious institute, a company, a political party, a trade union or a club: called 'imperatively coordinated association'. From this point of view dichotomy of positions exists in every association. In contrast with conflict theory, structural functionalism view society as a whole and each part of society is interrelated and interdependent with one another. But under conflict theory each organization is disintegrated from one another and position within each organization is dichotomized.

Conflict theorists suggest that there are 'authority relations' in every organization and people are constrained by a hierarchy of 'authority positions'. This means that people in authority positions are entitled to exercise control over other positions within the association. An individual in each association is either in subordinate position or in superior position. Since authority is attached to positions, a person who has different positions and roles in different organizations would have different levels of power. Conflict theorists recognize that the differential distribution of power in institutions which under certain conditions would result in the formation of 'conflict groups'. Often there is a conflict of interests between different social roles endowed with expectations of domination or subjection. It is because people who are in dominant positions want to maintain their status quo while those who are in subordinate positions want to take over. It is believed that people belonging to different positions would behave in the expected manner at the beginning. These groups of people are called 'quasi groups' and possess predetermined role interests along with their unconscious interests, called latent interests. Over time, these groups of people become aware of their latent interests; they would manifest their interest and form an 'interest group' and gain capacity to engage in group conflict. It has been pointed out that people who are in quasi groups are changed into interest groups must undergo several conditions.

For example, procedural condition is needed for developing interest group such as a leader to create interest group. Political condition such as the democratic and liberal political environment is also essential. Finally, the social condition requires enough communication available for people who are working together or being recruited in a similar way. All these conditions are necessary for the 'interest group' and 'conflict group' to materialize. On the contrary, since structural functionalists portray society as functionally integrated system and each part performs its functions for the other, each part can cooperate with each other in order to meet the needs of the whole social system. Even though people hold authority in their position, they would use their power for the benefit of others. This means that people would not use their power for their own ends, but use it to meet the needs of the whole social system.

Conflict theorists believe that the function of group conflict is to facilitate the development of democratic framework and acts like a catalyst in the process of change and development. It is because people who are in superior positions would have a chance to abuse their authority over others and forming a conflict group is a way to prevent them from abusing their power. The nature of conflict can be violent/ aggressive or intense/ extreme. Aggressive conflict involves the use of some kinds of weapons while intense conflict involves energy expenditure and high degree of involvement of conflicting groups. When the conflict is anticipated and written down, they are less violent and intense. This kind of conflict is institutionalized and this action helps to bring changes of the existing system. Therefore, once conflict groups are formed, people would engage certain actions such as demonstration, negotiation, petition, strike that lead to changes in social structure. In contrast with conflict theory, structural functionalism portrays society as stable and equilibrium. Although sometimes there is disorder in one part of society, the other part of society will help bring back equilibrium. This means that tension exists in one part can be released by the other parts of society. Therefore, society is always stable and in a state of moving equilibrium under the viewpoint of structural functionalism.

From the point of view of conflict theory, enforced constraint or coercion is the way to make social organizations fit together and maintain society's order. This means that people holding legal authority positions can give their sanctions against those who do not comply with them. Therefore, order and consistency in society are maintained by coercion under the viewpoint of conflict theory. But under the structural functionalist point of view, value consensus and social control are the key mechanisms to maintain society's order and consistency. This approach is focusing on how norm and value are internalized into people's own principles through the process of socialization and social control is a second line of defense to ensure people's behavior conforms to the society.

Both structural functionalism and conflict theory use macro level analysis to study social structures and institutions of society and offer two different angles for analyzing the changes in large-scale social structures and institutions of society. Structural functionalism views society as functionally integrated system that holds in equilibrium while conflict theory emphasizes on disintegration process of society due to the conflict of interest in all organization and at all time and society which is subject to social change. It is obvious that structural functionalism portrays the social world as stable and synchronized while conflict theory portrays the social world as unstable and discordant. Unlike functionalists, conflict theorists examine the manner in which different interests in society work against one another. Karl Marx, for example, demonstrated that the worker class and the capitalist class were necessarily in conflict over just about everything that went on in society, from the organization of work to the proper use of police and courts to the workings of a free press. But conflict also occurs between social institutions.

However conflicts may occur on other domains as well. The political scientist Stein Rokkan defines three different types of conflicts. These three types of conflicts are ideological, functional and territorial. An ideological conflict intends to decide the major identity of the human being. Functional conflicts are between interest groups and a territorial conflict occurs between the centre and the periphery.

Since the early 70's two new strands of theory and empirical research have arisen. The first, called *Resource Mobilization Theory*, takes as its starting point a critique of those theories that explain social movements as arising from conditions of social conflict and strain. By contrast, resource mobilization theorists argue that the origin and evolution of social movements rests mainly on the resources that are available to it. This implies forming new coalitions with existing organizations, securing financial support, and mounting effective and organized campaigns through political pressure. The other theory is called the *New Social Movement Theory*. It originates from an intellectual dissatisfaction with the predominantly Marxist view that reflects social movements as a fundamental struggle among classes organized around economic production. From their point of view this has become less relevant as these classes have been exposed to collective bargaining, the welfare system, and other socio-economic advancements of agents.

The relation between the social and economic conflict is close but not mechanical and can go in either direction. Traditionally, economic models have taken effective property rights as parametric and have been concerned only with analyzing the allocation of resources among productive uses and the distribution of the resulting product. But, this formulation of the economic problem is incomplete because it neglects the fact that the predatory activities by which agents create the effective property rights that incorporates allocation and distribution are themselves an alternative use of scarce resources. One has to extend standard economic analysis to allow the uses of scarce resources to include predatory activities as well as productive activities. The conventional core question of economics that, 'how do people interact to determine the allocation of scarce resources among alternative uses and the distribution of the resulting product', is to be rebuilt from the new perspective. To do so one has to extend the analysis of individual choices and social interactions incorporating the study of conflict. Economic conflict may arise in a variety of contexts and forms: conflict over claims to property, conflict between commoners and predators, civil and class conflict and the conflict between ruler and subject in a proprietary state.

Economic development involves appreciable change in a fundamental way. It involves economic actors taking actions that break from previous behaviours and an environment in continuing flux because of the reorientation that is going on. Of course the rate and effectiveness of the needed changes in socio-economic structure, as well as the vitality and effectiveness of efforts to adopt and master new forces, depends on the institutional structures supporting and molding economic activity, and the extent to which they facilitate productive change.

One gains profound insight from the existing theories of social and economic conflict to understand the origin and evolution of the torrent of changes that took place during the 21st century in the state of West Bengal. In the context of present scenario the following issues are to be addressed carefully. The answers would have a significant implication for West Bengal's social and economic change forthcoming in the future.

- *Understanding conflict*
  1. Modeling conflict: social-economic-political
  2. Group formation
  3. Social and economic structure of conflict
  4. Social and economic consequences of conflict
- *Measurement*
  1. Inequality and polarization
  2. Social exclusion and discrimination
  3. Social and economic mobility
- *Agreements under conflict*
  1. Right and might in agreements
  2. Institutional arrangements to lessen conflict
  3. Political systems and conflict of interests

References

1. Ralf Dahrendorf: Class and Class Conflict in Industrial Society, 1959.

2. W.W. Rostow: The Stages of Economic Growth: A Non-Communist Manifesto, Cambridge University Press, 1960.

3. N. Smelser: Mechanisms of and Adjustments to Change, in T. Burns (Ed.), Industrial Man, Penguin 1969.

4. James Farganis: Ralf Dahrendorf: Social Structure, Group Interests, and Conflict Groups, pp. 271-90 in James Farganis (Ed.), Readings in Social Theory, New York: McGraw Hill, 1996.

5. Jack Hirshleifer, The Dark Side of Force: Economic Foundations of Conflict Theory, Cambridge University Press, 2001.

10

Growth, Regional Pattern and Performance of Food-Processing Industry in West Bengal

Debnarayan Sarkar, Madhuchhanda Saha and Indrani Basu

Between 1950-51 and today, the production of food-grains has risen by 350%. In West Bengal, the production of food-grains has registered an increase from 1980-81 to 2000-01 with some in between fluctuations. However improved storing and post harvest processing facilities are needed to prevent a large part of this produce from being wasted. This demonstrates the need for massive growth of the virtually non-existent *Agro and Food Processing Sector.*

The country has about 20% middle class households. This class has more discretionary income to spend on quality processed food. They demand quality food products with wider variety, improved safety, with less negative environmental impact and greater convenience. Apart from growing middle class urbanization, increasing number of women in job market, rise in per capita income, convergence of consumer's food habits and the enormous reach of the national television network are the other key side drivers of growth of the food processing industries. Assessed on the basis of these parameter, food industry in India can play a vital role in enhancing rural income and employment through agricultural diversification, commercialization and value addition. The food industry has the potential to convert the subsidy-driven agriculture into a value-driven business, as multiplier effect of the industry is very high.

The agro products and food processing industry ranks fifth in the country in size and employs 16 lakh workers which consist of 20% of the country's industrial labour force. It accounts for 15.19% of the total industrial output with 5.5% of the GDP.

In spite of this, the food processing sector in India is extremely decentralized with processed food accounting for only around 2% of India's food output. At present, 1.3% fruits and vegetables produced in India are used by the processing industry. 75% of these products are consumed in domestic market. A big amount of fresh fruits are wasted as it can not reach the market on time. The $70 billion Indian Food Processing Industry is characterized by the predominance of small and tiny units spread all over the country.

Till 1980, industrialization in India was largely influenced by the Nehru-Mahalanobis model of development, which emphasized on developing the large-scale industries for the capital goods sector, and labour intensive and capital saving small industries for consumer goods sector. Post 1985 period witnessed a substantial change in the government policy towards technology imports and role of private foreign capital in the agro-industrial development. To give boost to its development, a separate ministry, i.e. Ministry of Food Processing Industries was set up in July, 1988. Further, the new policy initiatives commenced during July 1991 and thereafter in the form of liberalisation, privatization and globalisation (LPG) have provided new opportunities as well as challenges to this industry .

The present study attempts to make an assessment of the status of food-processing industry in the state of West Bengal. The specific objectives are:

(1) To assess the overall status of development of the food-processing industry in the state of West Bengal between 1980-81 and 1997-98 on the basis of certain selected indicators and examine its relative impact.

(2) To examine the inter-district disparities of its growth performance.

(3) To compare the relative efficiency score of different industries with reference to the food-processing industry.

This study has been divided into seven chapters. Chapter-2 provides the data set and methodology of this paper. Chapter-3 presents a brief overview of some unique features of the food processing industry. It also contains the pre and post-reform profile of the industry. Chapter-4 assesses the growth pattern of the industry vis-à-vis other industries on the basis of the annual compound growth rates. Inter-district comparisons are made as well. Employment, Net Value Added and Fixed Capital Interface are discussed in Chapter-5. In Chapter-6, the relative assessment of the food processing industry in relation to other industries has been studied. Finally Chapter-7 presents the concluding remarks.

2. Data and Methodology

The study is based on time-series data, collected from Statistical Abstract (2001-2002), and various issues of Economic Review published by the Government of West Bengal. District Statistical Handbook (DSH) published by the Bureau of Applied Economics and Statistics (BAES), Government of West Bengal, for each district also contains useful information. Inter-district comparison has been carried out on the basis of the number of units. It is worth mentioning that inter-sub-sector comparison could not be carried out due to non-availability of data.

Researchers have developed various production frontier models to compute efficiency and productivity of decision-making units (DMUs). Broadly, these models are categorized as deterministic and stochastic. The major weakness of the stochastic approach is the assumption (actual imposition) of an explicit functional form for the technology. Deterministic (Non-parametric) approach, on the other hand, does not require any assumption of the functional form. Some studies doubt about yielding similar results in respect of efficiency in all functional forms for the stochastic frontier production function (Brown,1957; Krishna and Sahota,1991; Banik,1994). In keeping with these features, we however, attempt to use non-parametric approach for measuring the efficiency of individual industries under our sample. More importantly, Farrell (1957) carried out the first empirical study to measure technical efficiency for a cross-section of firms by using DEA approach under deterministic (non-parametric) frontier approach. He dichotomized efficiency into technical and allocative efficiency. Technical efficiency reflects the ability of an industry to obtain maximum output from a given set of inputs. Allocative efficiency points to the ability of an industry to use the inputs in optimal proportions given their respective prices. These two measures are then combined to provide a measure of economic efficiency. Following Farrell (195), Aigner and Chu (1968), Timmer (1971) Charnes et.al., (1978) Banker el. (1984) and others extended this approach.

Despite the extension and development of stochastic frontier approach, deterministic frontier approach was later generalized to multiple outputs and reformulated as a mathematical programming problem by Charnes et.al.,(1978,1979,1981) thus initiating the mathematical programming approach to efficiency measurement, known as Data Envelopment Analysis (DEA). In DEA, efficiency of a DMU is computed relative to all other DMUs with the simple restriction that all DMUs lie on or below the efficient frontier. DEA uses linear programming (LP) to estimate the efficient frontier. Those DMUs which lie on the frontier are regarded as relatively efficient and have scores of 1.00, whereas those which lie inside the frontier are relatively inefficient and have scores of less than 1.00 but greater than zero. Besides identifying the inefficient DMUs, a DEA assessment yields valuable by-products that can be used to determine a suitable course of action for improving the performance of the inefficient DMUs. While the model developed by Charnes et.al., (1978)assumes constant returns to scale (CRS), the model was subsequently revised for variable returns to scale (VRS) by Banker el., (1984). Our study presents one DEA model of technical efficiency following Banker et.al., (1984) with deterministic production frontier approach. This study also presents a non-parametric DEA to measure technical efficiency for each individual industry by VRS model instead of CRS model. This is mainly because, among others, CRS technology does not envelop the data as closely as VRS (Lovell 1993, p. 29).

DEA methodology is described as "mathematical programming model applied to observed data (that) provides a new way of obtaining empirical estimates of external relationships such as the production function and/or efficiency production possibility surfaces that are the cornerstones of modern economics" (Charnes et.al.,1978).Using DEA, it is possible to construct production frontier as well as to measure efficiency relative to the constructed frontiers.DEA truly envelops a data set; it does not 'nearly' envelops a data set the way most econometric models do.

Let us assume there are 'n' decision-making units (DMUs) to be evaluated. Each DMU consumes varying amounts of 'm' different inputs to produce 's' different outputs. Let the respective input and output vectors are denoted by

$$X= (x_1, x_2,\ldots\ldots\ldots\ldots\ldots\ldots,x_m)\varepsilon R^m_+ \text{ and}$$

$$Y= (y_1, y_2,\ldots\ldots\ldots\ldots\ldots\ldots,y\text{-}_s)\ \varepsilon R^s_+ \text{, where}$$

R^m_+ and R^s_+ denote positive orthants of 'm' dimensional input and 's' dimensional output space respectively.

DEA analysis requires the solution of the following linear programming problem in Envelopment form:

$$VRS_E(Y_1, X\text{-}_1)$$

$$\text{Min } -(\Sigma s_r + \Sigma e_i)$$

$$\lambda_{1,}\ s_r,\ e_i$$

$$s_r \geq 0; r = 1, 2,\ldots\ldots\ldots\ldots, s$$

$$e_i \geq 0; i = 1, 2,\ldots\ldots\ldots\ldots, m$$

Turning to the multiplier side,

$$VRS_M(Y_1, X_1)$$

$$\text{Max } \Sigma y_{r1}\text{-}\Sigma x_{ij} v_i + w$$

$$\mu_{r,}\ v_i,\ w$$

Sublect to : $\Sigma y_{r1}\mu_{r\text{-}} - \Sigma x_{\text{-}ij} v_i + w \leq 0$ for j=1, 2,.......n

$\mu_r \geq 1$ for r=1, 2,.......s

$v_i \geq 1$ for I=1, 2,.......m

The optimal solution to $VRS_E(Y_1, X_1)$ for DMU_2 consists of s-vector output slacks, s_1, the m-vector excess inputs e_1 and n-vector λ_1.

The optimal solution to $VRS_M(Y_1, X_1)$ for DMU_1 is given by s-vector μ_r, the m-vector v_i and the variable w. In literature these values have been interpreted as virtual multipliers. Regarding the characterization of efficiency, a DMU is said to be efficient if it lies on the facet defining hyper-plane $\mu_1 y - v_1 x + w_1 = 0$ of the envelopment surface; whereas inefficient DMU lie below the closest supporting hyper-plane.

3. 1. Food Processing Industry in West Bengal: Some Unique Features

Before proceeding with the analysis of the problem and prospect of the food processing industry in West Bengal, it is important to take a look at some unique features of the industry.

The agro products and food processing industry ranks fifth in the country in size and employs 16 lakh workers, which consist of 20% of the country's industrial labour force. It accounts for 15.19% of the total industrial output with 5.5% of the GDP. West Bengal is well placed to spearhead the Food Processing revolution because its fertile soil, abundant water and favorable climate are ideally suited for the production of a wide range of fruits and vegetables. The food industry has the potential to convert the subsidy-driven agriculture into a value-driven business, as multiplier effect of the industry is very high.

In spite of this, the food-processing sector in West Bengal is decentralized with processed food accounting for only around 2% of the food output. At present, 1.3% fruits and vegetables produced in India are used by the processing industry.75% of these products are consumed in domestic market. A big amount of fresh fruits are wasted, as it cannot reach the market on time. The $70 billion Indian Food Processing Industry is characterized by the predominance of small and tiny units spread all over the country.

West Bengal offers exciting and profitable avenues for private investment in the area of Food Processing Industries. In a report released to the CII Partnership Summit, the Government identified some areas where projects in the state would have an edge. These include areas of Mushroom Cultivating and Processing, Dehydrated and Canned Fruits and Vegetables, Potato Processing and Frozen Fruits and Vegetables. There is also immense scope in the area of improved post harvest techniques to reduce losses in agriculture produce, which have been estimated at a high 30% of all production.

In a paper presented at the workshop on Investment Potential in Agro Processing Industries in Eastern India, organized by Bengal Chamber of Commerce and Industry and the Indo-German Chamber of Commerce, it was found that for food processing industries, there lies tremendous scope for private participation. The growth of Food Processing Industry will bring immense benefits to the economy, raising agricultural yield, creating employment and raising the standard of life of a very large number of people throughout the country, especially in the rural areas.

3.2. Pre and Post-reform Profile of the Industry

The agro-food industry can play a vital role in value addition and employment generation in agricultural and allied-agricultural sectors. The Tenth Plan focuses on promotion of investment in the industry and enhancing production, employment and exports ; providing adequate infrastructure and institution building ; and promotion of new technologies. It targets to augment food-processing level from the current 2% to 10% by the end of its period (GOI, 2002). This section presents the profile of the food industry vis-à-vis other industries in the pre and post-reform period with the purpose to examine how this industry has performed in comparison to other industries during the reform period.

Table- 1 shows that 62.25% of all registered factories in West Bengal during the pre-reform period (1980-81 to 1990-91) were agro-based. These agro-based firms contributed to about 48.75% of total organized industrial sector employment and 27.91% NVA by utilizing only 12.35% FC of the total organized industries. Although the share of agro-industry in terms of number of enterprises, FC and NVA has declined during the post-reform period, its share in INV capital and employment has increased. This indicates the enlargement of the industry, the capital intensification and labor displacing features of the industry. Comparing the agro-food industry to non-agro food industry, it is observed that food industry performed better than non-food industry in the post-reform period. The share of food industry in total and the industries under codes 20-21 are considered; here we witness a remarkable progress of the industry in terms of FC, employment and NVA. The table reveals that in spite of enhanced share of food industry in total capital usage during the post-reform period, the industry continues to be relatively labour-intensive and capital-saving as it comprises 12.43% employment of the total organized industries with only 2.95% of FC and 3.70% of invested capital.

To examine the performance of the food industry vis-a -vis other industries, key structural ratios are calculated and presented in Table-2. The Table shows that FC, employment and NVA per factory in food-industry have remained much lower than that of other industries in both the periods. However, these variables (FC, employment and NVA) themselves cannot stand as wholesome indicators of the performance of the industry. They require to be supplemented by FC/NVA, FC/EMP, NVA/FC and NVA/EMP ratios. The perusal of these ratios reveals the following:

(1) FC/NVA ratio in the food industry has increased in the post-reform period. This reveals that FC requirement per unit of NVA in the food industry has increased substantially in the post-reform period. Nevertheless, comparing the FC/NVA ratio of food industry to that of non-food industry , it is found that in both the periods, food industry has used relatively less FC per unit of NVA. For instance, as against 1.97 value of FC/NVA ratio in food industry, the value of FC/NVA ratio in non-agro industry is observed 3.65 in the post-reform period.

(2) The estimated capital-intensive ratio (FC/EMP) is lower in the food industry in both the periods. In pre-reform period, FC/EMP was only 0.29 whereas this ratio in non-agro industry was 0.94. However, in the post-reform period, FC per employee has increased significantly in all the industries including food-industry. This clearly evinces that after economic reform, entire industrial sector has become more capital intensive and labour saving.

(3) Capital productivity (NVA/FC) in food industry was more than double in relation to non-agro industry in both the periods. However, the capital productivity in food industry has declined significantly in the post-reform period. In a capital scarce country like India, declining capital productivity is not, likely, good for the economy.

(4) Labour productivity (NVA/EMP) in food industry was less than half of the productivity in non-agro industry. Comparing the pre-reform productivity of food industry with that of post-reform period, it is observed that the former has remarkably improved in the post-reform period. What are the causes of enhancement of intensive productivity during post-reform period ? Is it due to increase in education and skill of employees or due to less number of employees used per unit of FC ? As data about education and skill of employees in the food industry were not available, it would not be appropriate to draw conclusion that intensive productivity had increased due to education and skill enhancement of the employees. However, witnessing the fast growth of technical and professional education especially after economic liberalization and privatization of education, it is presumed that the average skill of employees in manufacturing sector has increased during the post-reform period. This might have improved the intensive productivity. Another cause, which is quite apparent from the FC/EMP ratio given in the Table, is the higher FC requirement per employee in the post-reform period. In a country like India where human resource is available in plenty, increase in intensive productivity on account of reduced capital-capital ratio rather than increase in skills of capital ratio does not appear to auger well for the economy.

Inter sub-sector comparison could not be carried out due to non availability of data at the district level. However we attempt to make an Inter – District Comparison (Table 3). This study confirms the process of rapid de-industrialisation in the State during the period under study. The number of units, on the contrary, has registered a small increase in the districts of Bankura, Kolkata, Murshidabad,Uttar Dinajpur and Dakshin Dinajpur, Malda and Cooch Behar.

4. Growth of Food-processing Industries vis-à-vis Other Industries

Annual compound growth rates (ACGRs) in number of firms, FC, invested capital (INV capital), employment and NVA have been estimated for the period 1980-81 to 1997-98 for all industries, agro-industries and separately for food and non-food agro industries. Table 4 highlights that agro-w at a rate lesser than that of all industries. Except employment and invested capital, in all the other characteristics, all industries have witnessed growth rates higher than that of agro-industries. Comparing the food and non-food agro industries, it is observed that the food industry has outperformed the non-food industry in terms of growth achieved in FC, invested capital, employment and NVA. Agro-food industry has shown a positive and significant growth rate in FC, invested capital and NVA, while insignificant rates are observed in case of number of units and employment. But agro-industries considered as a whole registered a significant growth in case of NVA, outperformed the non-food industry in terms of growth achieved in FC, invested capital, employment and NVA. Agro-food industry has shown a positive and significant growth rate in FC, invested capital and NVA, while insignificant rates are observed in case of number of units and employment. But agro-industries considered as a whole registered a significant growth in case of NVA.

Looking at the comparative growth of food and non-food processing sectors (Table 4), it is found that food-processing sector has become more capital intensive during 80s and 90s. The high growth rate observed in NVA has encouraged the producers to use more capital intensive and labour saving techniques. To examine the impact of NVA on FC and employment, regression analyses have been conducted by regressing employment and FC separately on NVA with a lag of one year, i.e., previous year's NVA affects the current year's FC and employment. The results are as follows :

$$EMP_t = 25233.3 + 1.9942\, NVA_{t-1}$$

$$(23157.8) \quad (1.1487)$$

$N = 6 \quad R^2 = 0.50113 \quad F = 3.0136$

$$FC_t = -13158.5 + 3.1793\, NVA_{t-1}$$

$$(13567.6) \quad (0.67301)$$

$N = 6 \quad R^2 = 0.88 \quad F = 22.3162$

where EMP = Number of workers (in thousand),

NVA = Net Value Added (Rs. Lakh)

FC = Fixed Capital (Rs. Lakh)

Figures in parentheses are standard errors of respective coefficients.

Regression coefficients are statistically significant. First equation shows that one unit increase in NVA in the previous year enhances the current year employment in food industry by 1.9942 units. The second equation shows that one unit increase in NVA in the preceding year causes an increase in current year FC by 3.1793 units. The regression results reveal that increase in NVA in the industry has positive and significant on FC and employment However, the impact is more on capital than on employment. This implies that a high growth rate achieved in NVA of the industry during 1980-81 to 1997-98 has increased the capital intensity in the industry.

As mentioned earlier, we could not carry out Inter sub-sector comparison due to non-availability of data at the district level and so we make an Inter-District Comparison. Table 3 clearly reveals that the food industry, as a whole, in West Bengal on the basis of the growth of number of firms did not achieve remarkable progress during the post-reform period.To study the regional pattern of the growth of the number of firms of the food industry (code 20-21) have been estimated in all the 18 districts. The growth rate represented in Table 5 shows that among all the districts only Murshidabad registered a positive growth in their number. All the other districts fell victim to the rapid process of de-industrialization during the period.

5. Employment, NVA and FC Interface

Since the inception of economic reforms in India, several studies have been conducted to investigate the effect of these reforms on employment generation in the organized manufacturing sector. After economic reforms, Indian industries have become more competitive. It was expected that they would downsize the workforce to improve their efficiency. This might lead to jobless growth in the industries. However, several studies conducted at national, State and district level reveal that employment has grown faster in post-reform period (Goldar : 2000, Singh and Agarwal :1999, Venkataramaiah and Burange : 2003). In food processing industry, except for Bihar and Uttar Pradesh, employment prospects in all other States have been better in the post-reform period as average number of employees was higher than that of pre-reform period.

To study the responsiveness of employment to the change in NVA and FC in the industry, regression analysis has been conducted using district level data for pre-reform period (average of 1980-81 to 1990-91) and post-reform period (average of 1991-92 to 1997-98). Due to problem of multi-collinearity between NVA and FC, we had to conduct bi-variate analysis in place of multi-variate analysis. The results are shown in Table 6.

The regression analysis based on aggregate data on agro-food industry shows that NVA has significant impact on employment generation in the industry in the pre-reform period. The value of the coefficients are statistically significant and values of R^2 and F are also high. However, it is observed that in the post-reform period, the value of coefficient is statistically insignificant. This implies that employment has no impact on change in NVA in the post-reform period. This is in line with the fact that after economic reform, entire industrial sector including the food industry has become more capital intensive and labour saving .

FC turns out to be significant in explaining variation when aggregate data are used. In both the periods, its coefficient is statistically significant . This implies that increase in FC raises employment in the industry. However, the impact of FC on employment has increased in the post-reform period as is evident from the higher value of its coefficient. Per factory increase in FC does not have any impact on per factory employment. This shows that it is not the growth of FC per factory, which has raised the employment in the industry ; it is the overall growth in FC that has increased volume of employment in the industry. This has happened due to addition of new factories in the wake of liberalization and globalization.

6. Relative Assessment

Efficiency is measured as the ratio of weighted output (virtual output) to weighted input (virtual input), and can take values between zero and one. Ideally one can treat industries with efficiency score equal to unity as efficient, while those less than one as inefficient. In other words, when the optimum values for the dual linear programs for any DMU possesses zero value, the DMU is efficient which lies on the envelopment surface. In Table-7, we present the relative efficiency scores of industries by efficiency levels.

Out of all these industries under our study, Textile Product, Wood and Wood Products, Leather and Fur Products (except repair), Gas and Stream are treated as efficient industries, as the efficiency score of each industry is one. Out of other industries, Manufacture of Wool, Silk and Synthetic Fibre Textiles, Manufacture of Chemical and Chemical Products (except Products of Petroleum and Coal), Manufacture of Rubber, Plastic, Petroleum and Coal Product, Manufacture of Machinery, Machine Tools and Parts (except Electrical Machinery), Other Manufacturing Industries, Repair Services also possess high efficiency scores ranging from 0.71 to 0.95.The industries of Manufacture of Jute, Hemp and Mesta Textiles and Water Works and Supply have a relative efficiency score of 0.5.Most interestingly, the food-product manufacturing industry was rather inefficient, as it possesses a relative efficiency score of only 0.04 the lowest efficiency being possessed by Basic Metal and Alloy Industries (0.03).

7. Conclusion

The study finds that the share of food-industry in total industries' invested capital and employment has increased in the post-reform period though its NVA has declined marginally. FC per unit of labour and per unit of NVA, though low compared to those observed in total agro-industry and total industry, has increased in the post-reform period, implying that the industry has become more capital intensive in the post-reform period.

Looking at the comparative growth of food and non-food industries, it is observed that the food industry has become more capital intensive. Increase in NVA has positive and significant effect on the capital intensity in the industry as is evident from the regression analysis that evinces that growth in NVA causes more increase in FC than in employment. This implies that a high growth achieved in NVA during 1981-82 to 1997-98 has increased capital intensity in the industry. The employment growth in the industry has been largely due to addition of new factories, not because of increase in employment intensity. The assessment of relative efficiency reflects that the food-industry did not perform well during the period under consideration. On the whole, West Bengal has experienced a downfall in performance of the industry.

This paper suggests that both the State Government and Corporate Sector should, jointly or individually, engage in direct investment for the establishment of agro-based industries in particular in those areas of West Bengal where the factors of production, especially raw materials, are available in larger quantities with lower unit cost of production. To this end, the State Government shall have to take up special initiative for infrastructural development and rapid progress of communication system and professional and technical education to support and enhance the industrial growth. The trade union should play their more crucial and responsible role in their own interest and also in the interest of their industries. More importantly, in order to pave the way for these programmes, the Central Government and the rival political and social groups must spread over their hand on the issue of industrial development of the state in the interest of the people of West Bengal as well as of India.

References

Aigner, D.J. and S.F. Chu (1968), "On Estimating the Industry Production Function", *American Economic Review,* Vol. 58, No. 4, September, pp. 826-839.

Banik, A.(1994): Technical Efficiency of Irrigated Farms in a Village of Bangladesh, *Indian Journal of Agricultural Economics,* Vol. 49, No.1, Jan-Mar.

Banker, R.D., A. Charnes and W.W. Cooper (1984): "Some Models Estimating Technical and Scale Inefficiencies in Data Envelopment Analysis". *Management Science*, Vol. 30. No. 9.

Brown, P.E.H. (1957): "The Meaning of the Fitted Cobb-Douglas Function", *The Quarterly Journal of Economics*, Vol. 71.

Charnes, A, W.W. Cooper, and E. Rhodes (1978) : "Measuring the Efficiency of Decision Making Units", *European Journal of Operational Research* 2(6) : 429-444.

Charnes, A, W.W. Cooper, and E.Rhodes (1979) : "Short Communication: Measuring the Efficiency of Decision Making Units" *European Journal of Operational Research* 3(4):339.

Charnes, A, W.W. Cooper, and E. Rhodes (1981) : "Evaluting Programme and Managerial Efficiency: An Application of Data Envelopment Analysis to Program Follow Through," *Management Science* 27(6):668-697.

Chengappa,P.G. (2004) : "Emerging Trends in Agro-Processing in India", *Indian Journal of Agricultural Economics*, Vol. 59, No.1, Jan-March

Farrell, M. (1957): "The Measurement of Productive Efficiency" *Journal of the Royal Statistical Society (A, General)* 120 (P.3): 253-281.

Krishna, K.L. and G.S. Sahota (1991): Technical Efficiency in Bangladesh Manufacturing Industries, *Bangladesh Development Studies*, Vol. 19, No. 1 and 2, Mar-Jun.

Lovell, C.A.K.(1993): Production Frontiers and Productive Efficiency, *The Measurement of Productive Efficiency: Technique and Application*, H.O. Fried, C.A.K. Lovell and Schnidt (Eds.) Oxford University Press.New York.

Pushpangadan, K.; Shanta, N. (2004) : "Growth and Efficiency of the Informal Sector in India: A Non-Parametric Analysis", *Labour and Development,* Vol.10, No. 1, June.

Sarker, D. and Sudipta, D.(2004) : "High Technical Efficiency of Farms in two different Agricultural lands: A study under Deterministic Production Frontier approach", *Indian Journal of Agricultural Economics*, Vol. 59, No. 2, April-June.

Singh, S.P. (2004): "Growth, Regional Pattern and Performance of Agro-Food Industry in India", *Journal of Rural Development,* Vol. 23(2), pp.121-154, Hyderabad.

Sinha, Sanjay, Sinha, Saurabh (1992) : "Small Scale Fruit and Vegetable Processing, Dynamics of Development", *Economic and Political Weekly*, June 27, 1992.

Timmer, C.P.(1971, "Using Probabilistic Frontier Production Function to Measure Technical Efficiency", *Journal of Political Economy*, Vol. 79, No. 4, July-August, pp.776-794.

Index

N